Third Edition

Tennis

STEPS TO SUCCESS

Jim Brown

Human Kinetics

Library of Congress Cataloging-in-Publication Data

Brown, Jim, 1940-
    Tennis : steps to success / Jim Brown.-- 3rd ed.
        p. cm. -- (Steps to success sports series)
    ISBN 0-7360-5363-8 (soft cover)
    1. Tennis. I. Title. II. Series.
    GV995.B6924 2004
    796.342'2--dc22

                                                    2004007825

ISBN-10: 0-7360-5363-8

ISBN-13: 978-0-7360-5363-1

Developmental Editor: Cynthia McEntire
Assistant Editor: Carla Zych
Copyeditor: Amie Bell
Proofreader: Julie Marx Goodreau
Graphic Designer: Nancy Rasmus
Graphic Artist: Tara Welsch
Cover Designer: Keith Blomberg
Photographer (cover): Dan Wendt
Art Manager: Kareema McLendon
Illustrator: Roberto Sabas
Printer: United Graphics

Human Kinetics books are available at special discounts for bulk purchase. Special editions or book excerpts can also be created to specification. For details, contact the Special Sales Manager at Human Kinetics.

Printed in the United States of America   10 9 8 7 6 5 4

Human Kinetics
Web site: www.HumanKinetics.com

United States: Human Kinetics
P.O. Box 5076
Champaign, IL 61825-5076
800-747-4457
e-mail: humank@hkusa.com

Canada: Human Kinetics
475 Devonshire Road, Unit 100
Windsor, ON N8Y 2L5
800-465-7301 (in Canada only)
e-mail: orders@hkcanada.com

Europe: Human Kinetics
107 Bradford Road
Stanningley
Leeds LS28 6AT, United Kingdom
+44 (0)113 255 5665
e-mail: hk@hkeurope.com

Australia: Human Kinetics
57A Price Avenue
Lower Mitcham, South Australia 5062
08 8372 0999
e-mail: liaw@hkaustralia.com

New Zealand: Human Kinetics
Division of Sports Distributors NZ Ltd.
P.O. Box 300 226 Albany
North Shore City, Auckland
0064 9 448 1207
e-mail: info@humankinetics.co.nz

Tennis: Steps to Success is dedicated to the memory of Bryan Kirby, a good tennis player, a good friend, and a good person.

JMB

◧ Contents

◩ Climbing the Steps to Tennis Success

For beginning and intermediate players, as well as teachers and coaches, this newest edition of *Tennis: Steps to Success* can help build a foundation or add to what the player has already accomplished in the sport.

The *Steps to Success* are arranged in order— one stroke at a time. Beginners can start with the forehand and backhand and learn to serve and volley before tackling specialty shots such as the half volley, lob, smash, and drop shot. The explanations and accompanying illustrations not only provide clear instructions for executing each stroke, but they also provide options. Players won't be locked, for instance, into a specific grip, stance, or swing. Experiment to find a style that fits your playing level, your body, and your attitude. The 10 percent of players who are left-handed get equal instructional treatment.

Intermediate players already know how to hit the ball. *Steps to Success* offers more thorough explanations of the strokes than do basic instruction books. Refine and polish skills with game-specific drills as you move toward playing at an advanced level. Get more insight into when and why to hit certain shots. Put the collection of strokes into a game plan that includes overall match strategy and point-by-point tactics.

For teachers, *Steps to Success* provides a turnkey instructional package. Teachers who already have an established teaching system can select from the information, drills, activities, and methods of grading that fit their programs. The background section includes a brief history of tennis, updated equipment information, an explanation of rules, warm-up and cool-down guidelines, information on tennis-related injuries and treatment, and Web-based tennis resources.

Then there are strokes, strategy, self-paced drills, and methods of evaluating each student, plus a 170-term tennis glossary. The previous editions of the book have been used in more than 100 colleges and universities, as well as in countless high schools. The approximately 80,000 people who have bought previous editions include teaching professionals, program directors, and parents working with their own children.

Tennis coaches, even those who were successful players, don't automatically acquire a complete understanding of strokes and strategy. Coaches add pieces of information to their personal databases step by step and year by year. *Steps to Success* can accelerate that learning process. This edition has "big-picture" strategy in each of the first eight steps and more than 200 tactical suggestions in steps 9 through 11.

For this edition, each step has been rewritten to include the best of past editions while adding new information; detailed explanations of stroke production; and instruction for beginning and intermediate players as well as some tips for advanced players. The instruction for each stroke also includes suggestions about overall strategy, and the last three chapters are devoted to specific tactics for almost every competitive situation. Better drills replace some of those from previous editions, and new drills have been added.

What could be new about tennis instruction? Plenty. As you will see in the section on equipment, racket technology continues to evolve. Lighter, bigger, stiffer, and stronger rackets allow players, regardless of skill level, to generate more racket speed and hit the ball harder. Young players are getting bigger and stronger. As a result, players can use a greater variety of acceptable stances, grips, and swings. Teaching methods have changed to keep up with the game, and those methods are reflected in every step.

The system of monitoring progress has been refined. There is a new way to score success for every drill and to determine an overall rating for each of the 11 steps. You'll know when you are ready to move on or what you need to work on before you do.

Steps to Success provides a systematic approach to playing and teaching tennis. Follow the same sequence as you work your way through each step:

1. *Stroke instruction.* In steps 1 through 8, read the explanations for executing the respective strokes and look at the accompanying illustrations to get a mental picture of how to hit the ball. These illustrated explanations include instruction for moving to the ball; holding the racket; and using the proper stance, preparation, swing, and follow-through.

2. *Self-paced drills.* Perform the drills within each step in the order in which they appear. Each drill can be modified to make it more difficult (see To Increase Difficulty) or less challenging (see To Decrease Difficulty), depending on skill level.

3. *Success checks.* While executing each drill, focus on a few components of the stroke. Read the Success Checks for a reminder of what to focus on.

4. *Score your success.* You will earn anywhere from 1 to 15 points on each drill. Repeat the drill as many times as you like, but don't worry about getting a perfect score. If you wait for perfection, you'll miss the fun.

5. *Missteps.* Players at all levels make some common errors on each stroke. Pointing out these missteps and offering ways to correct them may speed the learning process. If players are familiar with these common missteps ahead of time, they may be able to avoid them altogether.

6. *Success summary.* Near the end of each step is a Success Summary, a brief reminder of the most important teaching and learning points for that particular stroke. Each step concludes by asking you to rate your success. By circling the score you attained on each drill and adding up your points, you'll know if you need more practice or if you're ready to advance to the next step.

7. *Tactics.* Steps 9 through 11 answer some of the following tactical issues. How do singles tactics differ from those used in doubles? How do you prepare for the match? How do you play well against certain types of opponents? How do you adjust to various playing conditions? These three steps also contain drills and activities that simulate game and match situations.

Make *Steps to Success* work for you. Learn the game from scratch as a beginner, sharpen your skills as an intermediate player, teach the game using a systematic approach, or coach with a more comprehensive understanding of the game. Even advanced players will find drills that challenge their skills and strategy tips that might give them an edge over opponents.

The reward for completing the steps to success is whatever you want it to be. For some, playing tennis is just plain fun. For others, tennis provides a lifetime of healthy physical activity. And for those who like the competition, a world of players is out there waiting to challenge you. Good luck on this step-by-step journey to developing tennis skills, building confidence, and experiencing progress. Be sure to enjoy yourself along the way. Whoever and wherever you are, *Tennis: Steps to Success* is ready to take you several steps closer to becoming the best player you can be.

◨ The Sport of Tennis

Englishman Walter Wingfield had an idea he thought would make him rich. He combined the sports of badminton and court tennis to create lawn tennis, a game he first called *sphairistrike*, to be played on a court the shape of an hourglass. In 1874, Mr. Wingfield received a patent for his invention, devised a tennis kit, and put the kit on the market.

People took to lawn tennis quickly, although they did not subscribe to its Greek name or the shape of the court; and just as quickly, people realized they didn't need Wingfield's kit to play the game. He let the patent expire three years later, the same year a tennis tournament was held at the All England Club, the first Wimbledon. Although Wingfield never became rich, he is given credit for inventing a sport in which others have made millions and become sport superstars.

For a long time, tennis was a game played mostly by wealthy men who belonged to exclusive clubs. When the United States Lawn Tennis Association (now the United States Tennis Association, or USTA) extended its so-called protective wing to women in 1889, tennis became a respectable sport for both sexes. Female stars such as Suzanne Lenglen, Elizabeth Ryan, Helen Wills Moody, Alice Marble, and Helen Jacobs attracted fans—but men such as Bill Tilden, Jean Rene Lacoste, and Don Budge dominated play and headlines for the first half of the 20th century. Today, about half of the players in the United States are women, and many tennis fans think the women's game is more entertaining than the all-power all-the-time game played by the best male players in the world.

Club tennis is still strong, but people of all socioeconomic classes now play the sport. In the United States, most players participate free of charge on public courts. Most of the 22 million Americans who play tennis at least once a year range in age from 8 to 80 years old. Most are amateurs who play for fun with friends, in tournaments, on teams, and in leagues throughout the country.

Once only amateurs played tennis. When professional tennis finally arrived, the few players who could make a living, such as Richard

---

The Most Dominant Player Ever?

Who was the most dominant player in the history of tennis? Sampras? Williams? Laver? Navratilova? Borg? King?

Consider the case for Margaret Smith (Court). The Australian, born in 1942, won a total of 62 grand slam championships—more than anyone in history—in singles, doubles, and mixed doubles. She was only 18 when she won her first grand slam, the Australian Open. She took the grand slam in mixed doubles in 1963 and again in singles in 1970, for which she collected a total of $14,800. During that year, she won 21 of 27 tournaments. On three different occasions, she won singles, doubles, and mixed doubles titles at a grand slam event. She represented Australia six times in the Federation Cup and never lost a match.

Court retired in 1966, got married, and started a family. She returned to tennis in 1970 and won her last title in 1975. In 1991 she was ordained a Christian minister and founded a church in Perth, Australia.

Gonzales, Pancho Segura, and Jack Kramer, participated in small barnstorming matches and tournaments wherever a promoter could book an arena. Open tennis, in which professionals were allowed to compete with amateurs, started in the 1960s with the help of visionaries and promoters such as Kramer, Lamar Hunt, and George MacCall. Open tennis, however, was not a universally popular concept. An Australian newspaper demanded that MacCall, who was in Australia to sign the country's best players to professional contracts, leave the country. But open tennis was here to stay, and the game would never be the same again. The money paid to players, even to so-called amateurs, went from under-the-table deals to widely publicized contracts. Now world-class players often skip college to turn professional during their teens. In fact, the number of college graduates who have won major singles championships in the past 50 years can be counted on one hand.

Television changed tennis in ways both good and bad. In 1972, more than 50 million viewers in the United States watched Australian stars Ken Rosewall and Rod Laver play a classic. Rosewall won in five sets. A year later, Billie Jean King beat aging hustler Bobby Riggs in the "Battle of the Sexes" at the Astrodome in Houston, Texas. The spectacle attracted a crowd of 30,000 people plus a national television audience. American stars Jimmy Connors and John McEnroe played brilliantly in front of millions who watched on television, but it can be argued that their boorish behavior set an example that negatively influenced an entire generation of young players.

The number of players, products, and programs increased almost simultaneously with the growing number of tennis events shown on television. Names such as Ashe, Newcombe, Roche, Smith, King, Navratilova, Becker, Evert, Borg, Graff, Sampras, and more recently Agassi and the Williams sisters boosted ratings. The major tournaments—Wimbledon, the Australian Open, the French Open, and the U.S. Open—attract viewers who are not mainstream tennis fans.

Technology has also changed the sport of tennis. Once, courts were made only of grass, clay, or concrete. Now they are made of colorful synthetic products with made-to-order surfaces. Tennis rackets have gone from wood to graphite, boron, fiberglass, and Kevlar. The size of racket heads started at 60 to 70 square inches, moved up to jumbo-size models, and settled down to midsized and oversized frames of 100 to 115 square inches. The width of tennis rackets changed from narrow to wide and back again. Lighter, stiffer, and bigger rackets have made it easier for beginners to learn to play, for intermediate players to improve their strokes, and for pros to hit shots at bulletlike speeds. Serves have been recorded in the 150-mile-per-hour range.

Finally, the access to tennis instruction and the science of tennis training have changed. During the first two-thirds of the 20th century, interest was not high enough to support many teaching professionals. Today, however, tennis pros, teachers, coaches, camps, courses, and clinics are commonplace. Organizations and businesses train and certify people to become teaching professionals. The availability of information regarding preparation, performance, nutrition, hydration, psychology, safety, injury prevention and treatment, and sport science has, for the most part, elevated the quality of play. Unfortunately, little control is exerted on the quality of information, especially on the Internet, making tennis consumers vulnerable to fads, fiction, and frauds.

EQUIPMENT

All tennis players, regardless of skill level, require the same tools to play the game. Although their quality and cost may differ, rackets, strings, balls footwear, and tennis apparel are necessities of tennis life. Here are some suggestions for buying, using, and taking care of these products.

Rackets and Strings

When you shop for a tennis racket, take time to read the material on or attached to the racket. The labels, stickers, cards, and hangtags provide important information about racket-head size, length, string tension, flexibility, and other properties.

Wilson, Prince, and Head sell 75 percent of all tennis rackets. Approximately three-fourths of all tennis rackets are prestrung, are made of aluminum or low-end graphite, and cost between $20 and $90. For beginning players, rackets in the $50 to $90 range are just fine to get started.

The remaining 25 percent of rackets cost between $90 and $400 and are made of substances such as high-modulus carbon fiber, Kevlar, graphite, and even very small amounts of titanium, probably more for the marketing appeal than for racket performance. Intermediate players will want to upgrade to a racket in this category, usually in the $100 to $200 range.

When the first edition of *Tennis: Steps to Success* came out in 1989, rackets weighed between 11 and 14 ounces. By the time the second edition was published in 1995, racket weight had dropped to 9 ounces. Today rackets weigh as little as 8 ounces and as much as about 12.5 ounces. Beginners are better off with rackets that are on the lightweight side and relatively stiff (to provide power). Lighter rackets should have the weight distributed more toward the racket head. If not, players may find it very difficult to generate power. Nothing is wrong with heavier rackets, but they require the effort and skill of an intermediate or advanced player to be effective.

Generally, stiffer rackets provide more power, whereas flexible rackets are thought to offer greater control. Regardless of the flexibility of a racket or the lack thereof, controlling the ball is more a function of the player's skill than the type of racket. No measure of racket flexibility is universal. Each company has its own method of describing flexibility. Read the cards or hang-tags that are attached to new rackets, or talk to a salesperson who knows something about racket construction. Knowing what the different parts of a racket are called will help. Figure 1 illustrates everything from the butt to the tip.

As you progress along the steps to tennis success, you will develop a swing style. Players who have short swings seem to do better with stiffer rackets. Players with long swings prefer very flexible rackets. Other players have an intermediate-length swing, and they should look for a racket with intermediate flexibility.

Although racket weight has gone down, racket head size has increased, as mentioned earlier. Most rackets used to be 90 to 110 square inches. Now, the range is more like 95 to 115,

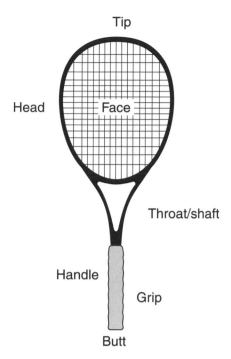

Figure 1　Parts of a tennis racket.

and most recreational players prefer those near the top end of that range. In a recent grand slam event, 13 of the top 20 men and women played with rackets with a racket head size slightly less than 100 square inches.

Grip sizes really haven't changed much during the past few decades. Each model comes in five or six sizes, ranging from 4 1/8 to 4 5/8 inches. The most common sizes are 4 3/8 and 4 1/2 inches. Look at the information on the racket near the top of the handle for the grip size. Here are several ways, none of them very scientific, to determine the correct grip size for your hand:

- Shake hands with the racket or hold it with an eastern forehand grip. As your fingers curl around the grip, the end of the thumb should touch the first joint of the middle finger (figure 2).

- Measure the distance from the tip of your ring finger to the long crease in the middle of your palm (the second line down from the base of your fingers). Position a ruler between your ring and middle fingers. The distance measured should be very close to the correct racket-circumference grip for your hands (figure 3).

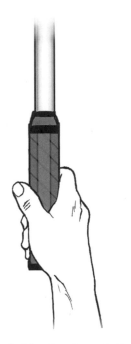

Figure 2 The end of the thumb meets the first joint on the middle finger.

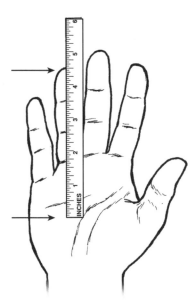

Figure 3 Measure from the tip of your ring finger to the second line in your palm.

- Hold the racket in your dominant hand. It should feel comfortable and easy to maneuver. The shape of the grip should fit the contour of your hand.

- Hold the racket in an eastern forehand grip. You should be able to fit the index finger of your nonhitting hand in the space between your ring finger and palm (figure 4). If there isn't enough room for

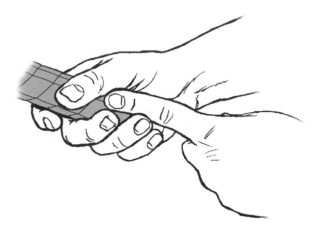

Figure 4 Fit the index finger of your nonhitting hand in the space between your palm and ring finger.

your index finger, the grip is too small. Conversely, if there is space between your finger and palm, the grip is too big.

- Play with a demo or loaner racket. If it twists in your hand on contact, the grip might be too small. If your hand and arm tire quickly, it might be too big.

Manufacturers have experimented with various racket lengths (up to 29 inches), but the average length has settled in at 27 1/4 inches. "Shorty" rackets are available for children and are a great idea for younger players learning the game.

Most rackets that cost less than $90 are already strung. Performance rackets—those that cost more and are used by intermediate and advanced players—are sold unstrung. The majority of players use nylon or other synthetic strings. The few who use gut (cow or sheep intestine) are either very good players or ones who are very serious about their games. Expect to pay from $20 to $60 for a string job. Again, look for a suggested string tension label somewhere around the racket throat. String tension ranges from 50 to 65 pounds. Generally, the lower the tension, the more power that can be generated. Tighter strings allow for more control, assuming you are a good enough player to control the ball regardless of racket flexibility and string tension. Try to settle on a string tension that gives you the best combination of power and control.

Unlike intermediate and advanced players, beginners don't usually break strings; they just play with rackets until the strings lose enough tension to affect power or control. How often should a racket be restrung? As many times a year as you play during a week. For example, if you play tennis twice a week, get your racket strung twice a year.

Once you have selected the right racket and strings, take care of them. Rackets endure a lot of abuse during the course of a lesson, practice session, or match. You can make them last longer and stay stronger by following these suggestions:

- Avoid storing rackets in hot, cold, or damp places.
- Keep racket covers on the rackets when they are not being used.
- Avoid spinning the racket on the court to determine serve and side.
- Don't use the racket to pick up balls if the frame scrapes the court.
- Wipe the strings clean after playing on a damp court or in high humidity.
- Use a replacement grip or overwrap when the original grip tears or becomes slick.
- Avoid tossing your racket, bouncing it off the court, or hitting things with it other than the ball.
- Check your racket for warping and cracks before getting it restrung.
- If a string breaks, remove all the strings to relieve tension on the frame.

Balls

The price of tennis balls hasn't changed much over the past 40 years. You can pay $3 to $4 for a single can of three premium quality balls at a tennis shop, or you can go to a mass merchandiser or sporting goods store and buy the same can of balls for $2.

Do not consider playing with cheap, low-quality tennis balls, even if you are a beginner. Buy the best ones available the first time out. Brand names can be deceiving, but Wilson, Penn, and Dunlop are three companies that make quality tennis balls. Whatever the brand, look for information on the plastic container indicating the balls have been approved by the United States Tennis Association or the International Tennis Federation.

Most balls are packaged in clear, plastic containers under pressure. If the pressure has not been maintained and the balls are soft when the can is opened, return the can to the dealer for a refund or a new can. If a ball breaks during the first two or three sets, take the can of balls back.

Three balls may last two or three outings for beginners and some intermediates, but after that they will begin to lose their pressure and bounce, or the felt will begin to wear off. When that happens, use them for practice only. Extend the life of balls by keeping them in the original container and by storing them in a cool place.

Ask for heavy-duty balls if you are going to play on hard surfaces. Regular (championship) balls are used on softer surfaces because they

When Strings Break Too Often

Broken strings are part of a tennis player's life, but what should you do when the rate at which racket strings break gets out of control? *Racquet Tech* magazine, a publication for professional stringers, noted that too many players quickly switch to a type of string made from Kevlar, which is durable but has a very stiff feel. Instead of making such a drastic change, David Bone, a stringing specialist, recommends taking several smaller steps, in the following order:

1. Use a thicker gauge of the same string.
2. Use string savers in the worn area.
3. Try a more durable construction of the same material in the strings that have been breaking.
4. Try a totally different material, but experiment with other synthetic strings before going to Kevlar.
5. Use a racket that has a denser string pattern.

don't wear as quickly. Tennis balls sold for play in high altitudes should be designated as high-altitude balls. Avoid taking heavy-duty or championship balls with you on a vacation to a high-altitude city. Instead, buy tennis balls when you get there.

Shoes and Socks

Discount stores sell affordable shoes that will get you through a tennis course or a series of lessons. But if you plan to play tennis three or more times a week, you should wear sport-specific tennis shoes.

Look for soft, flexible soles if you are going to be playing and practicing on soft, claylike courts. Even serious players can get months out of a pair of shoes on soft surfaces. Use tennis shoes with soles that are flexible and have added tread if you are going to play on hard courts, but don't be surprised if your shoes wear out within a few weeks.

Perhaps the most important feature of true tennis shoes is lateral control—that is, inside and outside stability. Tennis players spend as much time moving from side to side as they do going forward or backward. Choose shoes that will provide side-to-side motion control, preventing your ankle from rolling inward or outward and possibly helping you avoid ankle sprains. Other factors to consider are weight (buy the lightest shoes possible if other features meet your needs), comfort (walk, run, and change directions during the in-store test period), and cost (appearance and brand are not necessarily consistent with quality construction).

Tennis shoes get most of the publicity, but serious players know that the socks inside those shoes can affect performance and prevent injuries. Socks designed specifically for tennis players are thick or double-layered, with extra padding for the toe and heel. Some socks are so thick and cushioned you might have to buy shoes a half-size larger than usual. To repel sweat and expose it to the air for quick evaporation, the materials to look for in tennis socks are Coolmax, acrylic, polypropylene, and wool. Caution: Do not wear cotton socks for tennis. Not only are they poor in wicking moisture away from the foot, they also lose their shape, bunch up, and become abrasive quickly.

Apparel

The good news is that you can find moderately priced, high-quality tennis outfits at sporting goods, department, and discount stores, and at some pro and specialty shops. The bad news is that you can spend a lot of money on trendy shirts, shorts, skirts, warm-ups, and other active-wear clothing.

Students in high school and college activity classes usually wear shorts and shirts approved by the school. Dress codes may be in place, but no emphasis is put on fashion. If you take private or group lessons or compete in tennis events, there are guidelines to follow. A few facilities still require white attire, but most allow colors. Stay away from tank tops and swimsuits. Use common sense, observe what others are wearing, and ask somebody in charge what kind of dress is appropriate.

Most serious players practice in the most comfortable clothes they can find; T-shirts and baggy shorts are okay. They play matches in the best-looking outfits they can afford. More important than style, however, are clothes that are loose fitting for comfort of movement and light colored to keep you cool. In hot-weather months, consider wearing a hat. It will keep the perspiration from running down your face and give a little protection against harmful sunlight.

PLAYING A GAME, SET, MATCH

Singles is a *match* between two players; doubles is a match between four players, two on each team; and mixed doubles is a match pairing a man and woman on one team against a man and woman on the other team.

After a brief warm-up, the players decide who will serve first and on which end of the court. One of the players spins a racket in his or her hands or the players flip a coin. The ball is put into play by a serve, and the point is played out. *Points* are won when the opponent hits the ball into the net, outside the boundary lines, or does not hit the ball before it bounces twice.

After the serve, players may hit the ball before or after it has bounced on the court. One player serves an entire *game,* which may last from 4 points to an indefinite number of points. The server alternately serves from the right and left sides of the baseline to the receiver, who also moves back and forth from right to left to return the serve. A *set* is won when one player has won at least six games and is ahead by at least two games. The final score in a set might be 6-0, 6-1, 6-2, 6-3, 6-4, 7-5, 8-6, and so forth.

A player wins a match by winning two out of three, or three out of five, sets. When time is limited, pro sets might constitute a match. A pro set is won by the player who wins at least eight games and who is ahead by at least two games. Players change ends of the court when the total number of games played at any time during a set is an odd number.

In most matches, players are responsible for keeping their own score and for calling their opponents' shots in or out of bounds. No sound from a player means the shot is in and play continues. Shots that hit the lines are in play. Shouting "Out!" means the ball landed outside the boundary line and the point is over. In some tournament competition, an umpire may stand or sit near the net, call out the score, and settle disputes on close shots. At higher levels of the game, linespeople are positioned to make line calls. Figure 5 shows the lines and areas of the court.

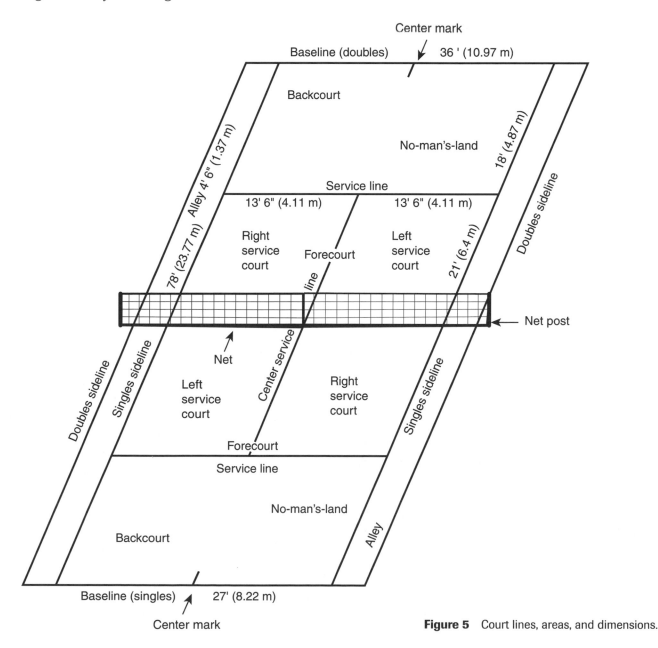

Figure 5 Court lines, areas, and dimensions.

A *match* may also refer to competition between two teams representing schools, clubs, or other groups. Within such a match there are games, sets, and points.

A tennis *tournament* involves teams or individuals competing against other teams or individuals in a series of matches. A high school or college team, for example, may enter a single-elimination tournament in which a team is eliminated from competition after one loss. The U.S. Open and Wimbledon are examples of single-elimination tournaments for the best players in the world. In a double-elimination tournament, which is rarely used in tennis, an individual or team that loses two matches is out. A round-robin tournament involves an individual or team competing against all of the other players or teams entered in that tournament. The team with the best overall win–loss record wins the tournament.

Singles Rules

Players take all practice shots before the match begins. Warm-ups are usually limited to five minutes. The player who wins the racket spin or coin toss may choose to serve or receive or decide on which side of the court to play the first game. The winner also has the option to make the other player choose first. The other player gets to choose whatever the winner hasn't chosen—that is, serving, receiving, or side of court. Read step 9, Competing As a Singles Player, for tactical considerations regarding these options.

To begin a game, the server stands behind the baseline to the right of the center mark and inside the singles sideline, facing the net. When the opponent is ready, the server has two chances to put the ball into play by tossing it into the air and hitting it into the service court across the net and diagonally opposite the baseline serving position. The server cannot step on or beyond the baseline before striking the ball.

The receiver is ready if he or she attempts to return the serve. The receiver can stand anywhere but must let the serve bounce before returning it. After each point, the server alternates between the left and right sides of the center mark to serve. If a served ball hits the top of the net and goes into the proper court, it is called a *let* and the serve is repeated.

You can win points if your opponent

- fails in both attempts to serve the ball into the proper court;
- hits the ball outside the proper boundary lines;
- hits the ball into the net;
- lets the ball bounce twice before returning it;
- reaches over the net to hit a ball before it has bounced;
- throws the racket and hits the ball;
- touches the net with his or her body or racket while the ball is in play;
- carries or catches the ball on the racket strings deliberately;
- does anything to hinder the opponent in making a shot;
- touches the ball with anything other than the racket during play; or
- touches or catches the ball during play, even if standing outside the court.

Players change sides of the court every time the total number of games played is odd. They are allowed 90 seconds to rest when changing sides (except after the first game of a set) and two minutes of rest between sets.

Doubles Rules

The server may stand anywhere behind the baseline between the center mark and the doubles sideline. The four players take turns serving an entire game. The order of serving stays the same throughout the set. In a game of AC versus BD, for example, A serves, then B, then C, and last D. Receivers decide who will receive serves on the right and left sides, respectively, and maintain that order throughout the set. Other rules described earlier for singles apply to doubles, except that after the serve, the alleys between the singles and doubles sidelines are in play.

Scoring

The server's score is always given first. Points are love (0), 15 (the first point won by either player),

30 (the second point), 40 (the third point), and game (the fourth point). If the players are tied at 3 or more points during a game, the score is called *deuce*. After deuce, when the server moves ahead by 1 point, the score is *ad in* or *advantage server*. If the receiver scores a point, it's *ad out*. A player must win 2 consecutive points after deuce to win that game. If not, the score goes back to deuce.

No-ad scoring was introduced to simplify the method of keeping score and to reduce the length of matches. In no-ad scoring, the first player to win 4 points wins the game. Points are 1, 2, 3, and game. When the score is tied at 3-3, the next point determines the game. At 3-3, the receiver chooses to receive the serve from either the right or left side.

It is much easier for casual fans and even for players to learn and remember a simple 1-2-3 system than the 15-30-40-deuce-ad method. Since no-ad scoring eliminates the requirement of having to win games by at least 2 points, the overall length of tennis matches can be reduced considerably. High school and college matches are usually played on unlighted courts after school and before dark. No-ad scoring allows matches to be completed during daylight. Also, tournaments with large numbers of players, a restricted amount of time, and limited court space frequently use this method of score-keeping.

The disadvantage of no-ad scoring is that the system penalizes the well-conditioned athlete. The player with good endurance can use longer games and sets to wear down an opponent. This doesn't happen as much in no-ad scoring. Because no game will last more than seven points, it may be possible for a player who gets a good start to gain an edge that cannot be overcome in a short match.

Tiebreakers were incorporated into the scoring system mainly as a result of television. With traditional scoring, the length of matches is unpredictable. Sets have lasted for 30 and 40 games, making it more difficult to sell advertising time and to manage programming schedules. Tiebreak games were introduced so a 6-6 set could end quickly.

Tiebreakers are scored as follows: In a 12-point tiebreaker, the player or team who wins

7 points, and is ahead by at least 2 points, wins the game and the set. The score is called out as 1, 2, 3, 4, and so on, throughout the game. A final tiebreak score might be 7-0, 7-1, 7-2, 7-3, 7-4, 7-5, 8-6, 9-7, and so forth.

The player whose turn it is to serve serves the first point from the right court. The opponent is the server for the second and third points. After the third point, each player serves alternately for 2 consecutive points until the winner of the game and set has been decided. The second server serves the second and third points from the left and right courts, respectively, and this alternating-serve system continues until the tiebreak game is completed. Figure 6 shows the rotation of servers and their positions.

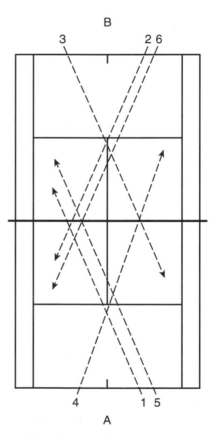

Figure 6 Tiebreak serving rotation.

Players change ends of the court after every 6 points and at the end of the tiebreaker, but no rest period occurs during the tiebreaker itself. The player or team who served first in the tiebreak game receives the serve in the first game of the next set.

Unwritten Rules

Because most tennis matches are played on the honor system without officials, some unwritten rules exist for players and spectators:

- If you ask someone to play a match, tennis balls are your responsibility.

- Take all practice serves before the first game begins, not when it is your turn to serve the first time.

- In unofficiated matches, keep your own score. The server should announce the score prior to each point.

- Each player is responsible for calling balls out on his or her side of the court. If you are in doubt, the shot is good. Never say, "Take two," to start the serving sequence over because you are not sure of whether a shot was in or out.

- Don't ask spectators to tell you if a ball is in or out. It's not their business, and they are not in a position to make a call.

- Play "in" shots. Immediately and loudly call all others "out." Never call shots "in."

- If a dispute arises about a line call, try to settle the argument with your opponent. If that doesn't work, ask for an umpire.

- If a loose ball on or behind the court interferes with concentration or becomes a safety hazard, call a "let" immediately and replay the point.

- If an unusual delay takes place between the first and second serves, allow your opponent to "take two."

- Don't shout at or distract your opponent in any way during a match. Not only is such distraction inappropriate, it's also against the rules. Furthermore, it is a sign of immaturity to groan, complain, curse, or verbally abuse yourself or others during a match.

- If one of your tennis balls rolls onto an adjacent court, wait for play on that court to stop before asking for your ball to be returned. Saying, "Thanks, court two," is one polite way to ask for help.

- When returning a stray ball to its court, wait until the point has been completed. Returning the ball immediately interferes with play.

- Shake hands with your opponent at the net after a match.

- If you are a spectator, hold your applause or cheers until a point has been completed. Tennis players react to sound and may stop a point if your noise is interpreted as a line call (such as "out" or "fault").

- Avoid walking behind a court during a point. Tennis players spend as much time between the baseline and the fence as they do inside the lines. Stay out of their way and their vision.

- Applaud or cheer well-played points and winning shots rather than errors made by a friend's opponent.

WARM-UP AND COOL-DOWN

The most common but least effective way to warm up is to hit balls. Although hitting balls is one way to get started, players using this method have a tendency not to exercise all of their muscles until actual play or difficult drills begin. Not warming up properly is an invitation to injury. A good warm-up period should prepare your body for strenuous activity without being tiring. Look at the warm-up as having two phases: a warm-up period and a time to stretch. Once you have warmed up and stretched properly you can practice hitting specific shots. After practice or play, take time to cool down. The cool-down allows your body to gradually return to a normal pace after strenuous activity. There is some evidence that stretching after a workout or match increases subsequent range of motion.

Start your general warm-up by moving around to increase blood flow. Try light calisthenics or jogging along the lines of the court. Jog around the court twice, for example, or combine jogging toward the net, backpedaling away from the net, and shuffling steps (one foot never crosses in front of the other) to move laterally across the court while facing the net.

After warming up, your muscles ought to be ready for some stretches. Hold each stretch for 10 seconds without bouncing and repeat each stretch two or three times. Include stretches for your upper body (towel stretch), trunk (standing or seated twist), and legs (lunge).

Now you're ready to hit. Start in the forecourt area and exchange soft, short groundstrokes with your practice partner. Next, move to the baseline and hit controlled forehands and backhands. Alternate roles with your partner to practice down-the-line groundstrokes, crosscourt groundstrokes, and volleys while your partner returns with groundstrokes.

Following the match or practice session, cool down by walking the perimeter of the doubles court for five minutes or until your pulse rate drops below 120 beats per minute. Then repeat your stretching exercises while your muscles are still warm.

TENNIS INJURIES

Tennis players get hurt. Although tennis elbow gets most of the publicity, several less serious, but more common, injuries occur among tennis players. Blisters, sprains, strains, cramps, and shin splints, as well as tennis elbow, are examples of problems almost all players encounter sooner or later (see table 1). In most cases, tennis injuries are not emergencies, and the player who has some information can take care of them personally.

Table 1 Injuries, Causes, and Treatments

Injury	Causes	Treatments
Blisters (irritated, fluid-filled portions of the skin)	• Racket-hand irritation • Foot, sock, shoe irritation	• If blister is not torn, keep surface area intact • Do not deliberately open blister • If blister is torn, clean and apply mild ointment • Apply liquid bandage product or bandage and tape
Sprains (stretched or torn ligaments)	• Forcing a joint beyond its normal range of motion	• Ice every 20 minutes for 24 to 48 hours • Compression • Elevation • Rest
Strains (stretched or torn muscles or tendons)	• Overexertion • Improper warm-up • Sudden movement • Fatigue	• Ice every 20 minutes during first day after injury • Heat before playing • Ice after playing
Cramps (violent, involuntary muscle spasms)	• Fatigue • Overexertion • Chemical imbalance • Dehydration	• Stretch affected muscle • Ice • Pressure • Massage • Fluids
Shin splints (front leg pain)	• Hard surfaces • Poor conditioning • Inadequate arch support • Poor running technique • Congenital problems	• Rest • Ice • Compression • Elevation • Appropriate footwear
Tennis elbow (inflammation of tendon of forearm muscle)	• Forearm stress • Weak muscles • Improper hitting technique • Wrong racket • Bone fragments	• Ice and massage • Moist heat after 72 hours • Aspirin or ibuprofen • Rest • Correct racket • Arm band or brace

Treating Tennis Elbow: Three Ways to Go

Tennis elbow, a repetitive stress condition affecting the forearm muscles, is still one of the most common and difficult-to-heal sports injuries. This condition affects as many as half of all frequent tennis players, but it can be just as debilitating to golfers, baseball players, volleyball players, and a variety of others who may never pick up a tennis racket.

"There are three treatment phases athletes have to consider," says Todd Ellenbecker, MS, PT, and clinic director of physiotherapy associates at the Scottsdale Sports Clinic. "Phase one is self-treatment, which often consists of rest, ice, NSAIDs (nonsteroidal anti-inflammatory drugs), sport creams, or possibly using a brace to alleviate the stress that aggravates the injury. Players in this group may try restringing their rackets or changing their swings on certain strokes. They might also try exercising with light arm weights. In some cases, these measures are effective and the person can resume participation without further problems."

If problems persist, the player moves to phase two and sees a sports medicine physician, physical therapist, or athletic trainer. "Heat, ice, ultrasound, iontophoresis, and electrical stimulation may be prescribed," continues Ellenbecker. "Low-resistance, high-repetition exercises are recommended for the wrist and forearm and, increasingly, for the shoulders and upper back. The player may also be advised to change a technique that causes the inflammation. Most physicians allow between 6 and 12 weeks to see if conservative treatment is going to be effective."

At phase three, the doctor may recommend a limited number of cortisone injections to quiet the inflammatory process. However, some of the country's most knowledgeable experts on the elbow think that some cases of tennis elbow are more degenerative than inflammatory in nature and do not think that anti-inflammatory substances will work.

A second alternative in phase three is surgery. The surgeon goes in and takes out the areas of a tendon that are, in effect, dead. Surgeons also create small holes in the area's bone tissue that encourage blood flow and helps the area to regenerate and heal.

Aside from these three phases of treatment, other alternatives are available to treat tennis elbow that are less than mainstream. One of these, electrocorporeal shock wave therapy, has been approved by the FDA and has about a 60 percent success rate. There are plenty of anecdotal accounts of successful acupuncture, but little scientific study has been done to support its success in treating this injury.

Serious tennis elbow problems will not go away by themselves. Decide which phase you are in, then make a decision whether to stay there or move on to a more aggressive approach that will allow you to resume training and competition.

RESOURCES

If you live in the United States and want to become more involved in the game, join the United States Tennis Association (USTA) (see www.usta.org). The USTA is the nonprofit governing body of tennis in the United States. Its mission is to promote and develop the growth of tennis. The USTA is divided into 17 sections, which are further divided into districts. Most USTA income is derived from membership fees and from sponsorship of the U.S. Open, played each year at the National Tennis Center in New York. USTA members can play in tournaments, receive publications, get professional instruction, and obtain other benefits of belonging to an organization with hundreds of thousands of members.

Following is contact information for other selected national tennis organizations, which offer similar benefits to their members:

Australia: www.tennisaustralia.com.au

Canada: www.tenniscanada.com

Great Britain: www.lta.org.uk

India: www.aitatennis.com

Ireland: www.tennisireland.ie

Mexico: www.fmttenis.com

New Zealand: www.tennisnz.com

Republic of South Africa:
www.supertennis.co.za

Founded in 1927, the United States Professional Tennis Association (USPTA, see www.uspta.org) is the world's oldest and largest association of teaching professionals. It has more than 12,500 members in the United States and other countries. The typical recreational player does not have direct contact with the USPTA, but its members make up one of the major tennis teaching organizations in the country.

The Professional Tennis Registry (PTR, see www.ptrtennis.org) is also a not-for-profit organization dedicated to informing, educating, and training tennis teachers. The organization was founded by Dennis van der Meer to educate, certify, and service tennis teachers and coaches around the world. PTR has more than 10,000 members in 120 countries.

Key to Diagrams

→   Running path

         Tennis ball or bounce of tennis ball

A   Player A   C   Player C

B   Player B   D   Player D

- - →   Path of tennis ball

F   Feeder

S   Server

R   Receiver

         Target area

SP   Server's partner

RP   Receiver's partner

Hitting Forehands for Offensive Control

Every tennis player needs a signature shot, that one stroke to call on when he or she really needs it. For many players, that stroke is the forehand. This stroke is the most frequently hit shot, the first one taught, and the easiest to learn. Consider the forehand the foundation for your game. Build a strong base with the forehand, and it will support all of the other strokes. The forehand can even be used to hide weaknesses in a player's game.

Some strokes just beg you to set them free. It's not easy to attack with a backhand groundstroke. Some players find it hard to set up points with a serve. Low volleys don't let you do anything but hope for another chance. But the forehand stroke is different, and you can develop it into your strongest weapon. Use the forehand to build points. Use it to take charge. Use it to move your opponent around the court and to confuse your opponent. Use it to extend points. And use the forehand to put winners away into an open area. Make a statement with your forehand that says, "Don't mess with me." Read steps 9 and 10 for point-by-point tactics using the forehand in singles and doubles play, respectively.

Before going into the details of the forehand grip, let's look at where to position oneself during the course of a point. In singles, the base of operations after the ball has been put into play should be on or just behind the baseline at the center mark (figure 1.1). When in doubt, take that position and return to it after each shot. The base will change during exchanges, depending on where the opponent hits the ball. More than once in this book, you will see references to bisecting the angle of possible returns. This direction is a semiscientific way of saying, "Stand in the middle of where you think the ball is likely to come." But for now, consider the spot at the middle of the baseline home base.

The forehand can be hit in many ways. This fact is good news because it means several options are available so that you can find a comfort zone and assume some of the responsibility for your playing style. Although most players have a basic forehand grip, they make slight changes in the grip during a point that they may not even be aware of or remember.

Every stroke in tennis consists of a sequence of separate movements—preparation, swing,

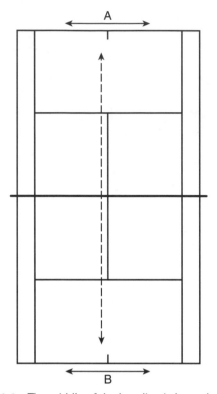

Figure 1.1 The middle of the baseline is home base between shots.

and follow-through. The trick is to make all these movements come together in one smooth motion. The forehand starts with the feet. Good tennis players have good footwork. By getting the feet to the right place on the court and lined up in the proper position, you're setting the stage for the combination of movements that concludes with a successful shot.

As your feet move to establish a hitting position, your hips and trunk get ready to transfer all that energy to your arm and racket. As you move the bottom half of your body into position, bring the racket back far enough to generate some power when it's time to hit. In other words, as you set up for the forehand, your whole body is winding up. Sometimes, you'll take a big windup; other times, you'll want to make it short and compact. This sequence of events peaks when you swing to strike the ball, and it finishes with the follow-through (figure 1.2). Starting now, everything you learn about the forehand should eventually help you hit with power, control, and confidence.

Figure 1.2   Forehand

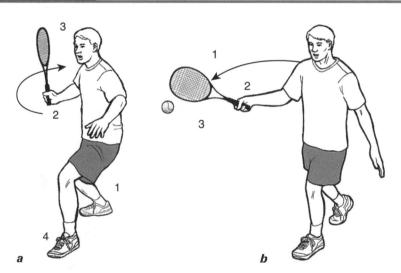

PREPARATION

1. Quick crossover or shuffle step to get to the ball
2. Eastern or semiwestern grip
3. Shoulder turn and racket back early
4. Square or semiopen stance

SWING

1. Up-then-down loop with racket head
2. Upward and forward motion
3. Early contact

FOLLOW-THROUGH

1. Hit through the ball
2. Up, out toward net, and across (for eastern grip)
3. Up and across (semiwestern or western grip)

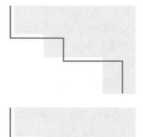

Misstep

Your swing is inconsistent.

Correction

Keep your wrist in a fixed laid-back position. The more movement in your wrist, the less control you will have.

Misstep

You are rushing the swing.

Correction

Start preparing to return a ball as soon as it leaves your opponent's racket face. Don't wait for the bounce.

For better or worse, players use four different forehand grips (continental, eastern, semiwestern, and western); assume four different stances (open, semiopen, closed, and square); and hit the ball with topspin, sidespin, underspin, or no spin. And we haven't even touched on back-swings, swing paths, hitting zones, and follow-throughs!

Don't be overwhelmed. Although all of these items will be illustrated and discussed, certain grips and stances are recommended. Beyond that, it's up to you. Some of these variations are not very practical or effective. Others can be added or incorporated into your game as it matures.

GRIPS

One constant applies to every forehand grip: Place the off hand (the nondominant one) on the shaft of the racket between shots. Use the off hand to support the racket while making slight adjustments with the dominant hand. Make using the off hand to adjust the grip an automatic response. One-handed grip changes don't work. Although we cover the continental and western grips in this section as well, the eastern or semiwestern grips are the ones recommended for the forehand.

Eastern Forehand Grip

With the nondominant hand, hold a racket at the shaft, perpendicular to the court. With the other hand, shake hands with the racket so that your palm rests against the back bevel of the handle. This grip is the eastern forehand (figure 1.3). Curl your fingers around the grip near its base. For a right-handed player who is holding the racket out to the right side, the wrist should be slightly to the right of the top, and the V formed by the thumb and index finger should be above but slightly toward the back part of the handle. A left-handed player should hold the racket so the wrist is slightly to the left of the top of the grip when looking down over the top.

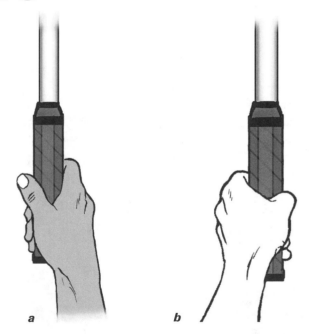

a b

Figure 1.3 Eastern forehand grip: *(a)* right-handed player; *(b)* left-handed player.

The eastern grip is the most traditional way to hold a forehand, but it is not used by many of the top players. It is problematic, however, when teachers instruct their students to grip a racket in the same way as elite players do, whether or not a different grip is appropriate for less-than-elite players. A majority of teaching professionals stay with the eastern forehand for beginners, but they allow students to migrate toward other grips as they become more advanced.

The advantages of the eastern forehand are the natural position of the wrist, greater reliance on the shoulder joint, less stress on the elbow and wrist, and an easier transition to net play. All are compelling arguments. The disadvantages are not being able to hit with maximum power on some shots, not being able to hit topspin as effectively as with two other grips, and not being able to respond easily to high-bouncing shots.

The eastern forehand grip is a reasonable, practical alternative for beginning, intermediate, and advanced players, but it is not well supported by teachers who work only with very good players. For these teachers, the semiwestern is the first choice for forehand grips.

Semiwestern Grip

Hold the racket with the eastern forehand grip. Now rotate your wrist to a position even farther behind the side of the grip. Think of the semiwestern as being halfway between an eastern and a western grip. (More about the western grip appears next.) With the semiwestern grip (figure 1.4), you can hit the ball harder than with the eastern, and it's easier to hit a ball with topspin. You can also strike the ball earlier and catch it on the rise.

But the semiwestern has its drawbacks. It may be harder for some beginners to master, it definitely is not a great grip for low-bouncing balls, and it's a terrible grip for net play. It is also a more difficult adjustment to go from a semiwestern to a grip that can be used at the net. The switch from an eastern forehand to a volleying grip is smoother. Some semiwestern grip players are never able to make the adjustment and stay on the baseline their entire game. If this grip is too uncomfortable, rotate your hand slightly back toward an eastern grip. All of that being said, the semiwestern still makes sense for a lot of very good players. Whether they started out with the grip or grew into it hasn't been studied.

Western Grip

Again, start with the eastern grip, with your wrist slightly to the right of the top of the racket handle. Move it more to the right until you have the semiwestern. Now, rotate your wrist one more turn until your palm is actually under the racket handle (figure 1.5). Does this grip feel weird? The western grip looks weird, too. But some players learn to play with the western forehand grip and are very successful with it.

The western grip is especially popular with players who stay on the baseline and hit from an open stance. It's great for hitting with topspin and for taking high balls, but that's about all. It is hard to hit low-bouncing balls and balls that go

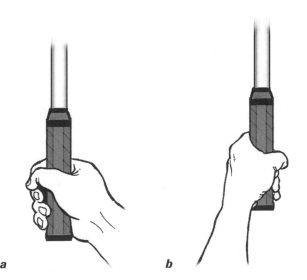

Figure 1.4 Semiwestern grip: *(a)* right-handed player; *(b)* left-handed player.

Figure 1.5 Western grip.

wide to the forehand side using the western grip. Western grip players also have a difficult time adapting to conventional grips for the volley.

Unless you have a compelling reason to use the western grip, don't. Occasions may arise during a point when shifting to a western grip will help you hit the ball with extreme topspin or allow you to hit one that bounces very high. Other than these occasions, you're better off with an eastern grip or a semiwestern grip.

Continental Grip

One more forehand grip should be mentioned—the continental grip (figure 1.6). As you did with the eastern grip, start by holding the racket perpendicular to the court and shaking hands so that your palm rests against the back of the handle. Instead of rotating your wrist to the right (for a right-handed player), move it a fraction of a turn to the left so that your wrist is directly on top of the racket handle. Extend your thumb along the grip so the inside part is in contact with the flat bevel. If you are a left-handed player, move your wrist from left to right out of the eastern forehand to a position where your wrist is aligned on top.

Got all that? Don't use it, at least not for forehand groundstrokes. There are better, more comfortable ways to grip the racket for this shot. But knowing how to hold a continental grip will be useful when you reach the steps on serves and volleys.

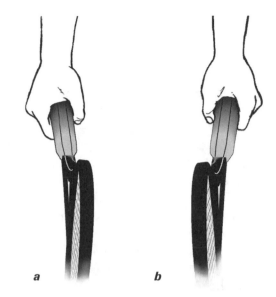

Figure 1.6 Continental grip: *(a)* right-handed player; *(b)* left-handed player.

Whatever grip you decide to use, several get-acquainted activities are recommended that require only you, the racket, and one tennis ball. The simplest activity is to dribble the ball on the court using the racket strings while holding the racket with the eastern or semiwestern grip. Dribbling the ball with the racket is something you'll do without even thinking about it for the rest of your tennis life, so you might as well get used to it now. To make things more interesting, dribble along any line on the court or turn your racket palm up and bounce the ball up instead of down. If you can do 100 up or down dribbles without a miss, you've got it. Move on to something else.

READY POSITION

The one thing that hasn't changed about the forehand is the ready position (figure 1.7). This is the position in which you stand in anticipation of your opponent's next shot. Assuming the ready position indicates that you are alert, poised for action, and watching the ball leave your opponent's racket.

In the ready position, your feet should be square to the net. Hold the racket in a forehand grip unless you expect the ball to go somewhere else. Flex your knees slightly and lean forward. Place your arms, hands, and racket up and extended forward comfortably. Focus your eyes over the top of the racket.

Figure 1.7 Ready position.

Regarding the most fundamental grip in the game, the forehand grip, there is a difference between what the great players do and what is taught at the grassroots level of tennis.

Miguel Crespo is responsible for the International Tennis Federation Coaches Education Program, and Jose Higueras has been an advisor to the USTA and has worked with players such as Michael Chang and Jim Courier. In *World Class Tennis Technique,* Crespo and Higueras wrote about the eastern forehand grip as though it were a relic of the past. The eastern grip, wrote the coauthors, is the traditional grip; whereas the semiwestern or western is the modern grip: "The semiwestern grip is recommended as the grip that players should use to play the modern forehand as it provides for the best transfer forward of both power and spin. We agree with this and further view the semiwestern grip as the preferred grip with the eastern and western grips being two varieties."

Yet, teaching professionals who either work with or supervise instruction for less-than-elite players will tell you that they typically start players with the traditional eastern forehand grip. Jim Coyne, USTA NorCal Junior Tennis director, says, "I may be old-fashioned, but I agree with those who teach the eastern grip. We might use a slightly open stance, but we start novices with a basic step forward toward the net. The eastern grip helps in transitioning later at the net and on the serve."

Coyne continues, "My experience shows me that although we start them with basic grips and stances, the players evolve into different grips and stances as they play more. I think we need to work up from the basics instead of telling beginners and intermediates to imitate world-class players."

Randy Chamberlain, who supervises a group of tennis instruction facilities in Minneapolis, agrees with Coyne. "When we get students who are at square one, we typically introduce the game using traditional principles. Kids exposed to tournament play and the pressure to hit big do gravitate toward the big western grip and open stance. Probably 80 percent of our teaching professionals are old school."

Dr. Paul Roetert, director of USA Tennis High Performance, offers a compromise: "When learning tennis, I would stay away from extreme grips. On the forehand side, I would consider an extreme western grip or continental grip difficult to use as a basis for the stroke. There is a range of grips in between, including the eastern forehand grip, which I would consider acceptable and helpful for future development."

So, what should you do? Start with the eastern forehand grip and change to the semiwestern grip only if it makes you a better player. Resist the temptation to go all the way to a western forehand grip, and don't even consider the continental for this stroke. You'll need the continental for serves, volleys, and overhead smashes.

FOOTWORK

Some returns require little or no movement. You just move the racket back and hit. On shots that are farther away from you, there are two ways to get to the ball. The first is a shuffle step (figure 1.8). Move laterally right or left, sliding your feet alternately in the direction you want to go. While you're shuffling, get the racket back in a position to pop a forehand. Keep your hips low to the ground by bending at the knees.

The other method of moving to the ball is called a crossover step (figure 1.9). The crossover step is used to run for shots farther away.

The technique is simple: To move to your right, turn your right foot, then cross over with the left and take off. To move to your left, pivot the left foot and cross in front with the right one. It doesn't matter if you are right-handed or left-handed. The technique for the crossover step is the same.

The following footwork drills will help improve footwork skill. Once you can move from side to side quickly and without even thinking about footwork, you're ready to concentrate on other fundamentals.

Figure 1.8 Shuffle step.

Figure 1.9 Crossover step.

Footwork Drill 1. *Grounders*

To practice court coverage, start with grounders (figure 1.10). Stand at the center mark without a racket but in ready position. A practice partner stands at the T, where the center service line intersects the service line, holding two tennis balls. Your partner rolls the balls alternately to your right and left sides for a total of 10 times, 5 to the right and 5 to the left. Using the shuffle step, move to the right to field the first grounder, roll it back to your partner, and shuffle to the left for the next ball.

A variation of the grounders drill is the wave. Start at the center mark on the baseline. Have a practice partner or teacher stand 20 feet in front of you and signal you to move forward, backward, right, or left. Carry the racket in the ready position and use the shuffle step to move right and left. Continue for 30 seconds then change roles.

Figure 1.10   Grounders.

To Increase Difficulty

• Partner tosses grounders randomly to the right or left.
• Partner increases the speed of the ball.
• Partner increases the distance between grounders.

To Decrease Difficulty

• Partner tosses grounders only to one side.
• Partner slows the speed of the ball.
• Partner narrows the distance between grounders.

Success Check

• Shuffle and slide without crossing your feet.
• Keep your hips low to the ground.

Score Your Success

1 to 3 grounders fielded without a bobble = 1 point

4 to 7 grounders fielded without a bobble = 3 points

8 to 10 grounders fielded without a bobble = 5 points

Your score ___

Footwork Drill 2.   *One-Bounce Catch*

For the one-bounce catch drill, you and a partner take the same positions as in grounders. Instead of rolling grounders to you, your partner alternately tosses 10 balls so that they bounce to your right and left. Take a crossover step, move quickly, and catch the ball with one hand before it bounces a second time (figure 1.11). Roll it back and recover to a ready position for the next toss. Tosses can be thrown to bounce at about waist height along the baseline, behind it, or in front of it.

Figure 1.11   One-bounce catch.

To Increase Difficulty

- Partner tosses balls randomly to the right or left.
- Partner increases the speed of tossed balls.
- Partner increases the distance between tossed balls.

To Decrease Difficulty

- Partner tosses balls only to one side.
- Partner slows the speed of tossed balls.
- Partner narrows the distance between tossed balls.

Success Check

- Do a quick pivot and crossover step.
- Plant the outside foot and push off for the next catch.

Score Your Success

1 to 3 balls caught after one bounce =
 1 point

4 to 7 balls caught after one bounce =
 3 points

8 to 10 balls caught after one bounce =
 5 points

Your score ___

Footwork Drill 3. *Shuffle-Crossover Step*

Take a ready position in the middle of a service court. Carrying a racket, use a shuffle step to move past the singles sideline as fast as you can. Plant the outside foot, and use a crossover step to turn and run past the centerline. Return to the starting point and do the same thing in the opposite direction until you've completed a total of 10 back-and-forth movements (figure 1.12).

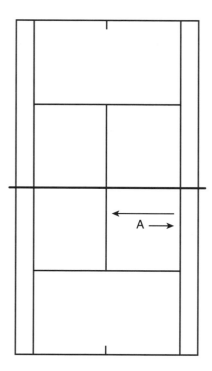

Figure 1.12 Shuffle-crossover step.

To Increase Difficulty

- Don't stop between drill segments. Keep moving until you finish 10 sequences.
- Have a partner time the first segment. Try to match or break your speed record with each subsequent trial.

To Decrease Difficulty

- Move at a slow-motion speed to practice the footwork.

Success Check

- Stay low to maintain your center of gravity.
- Plant the outside foot to push off when changing directions.

Score Your Success

1 to 3 perfect footwork sequences = 1 point

4 to 7 perfect footwork sequences = 3 points

8 to 10 perfect footwork sequences = 5 points

Your score ___

STANCE

Four options are available for positioning your feet—square, closed, semiopen, and open—and you'll probably use all of them sooner or later. The four options are described next.

The *square stance* (figure 1.13), sometimes referred to as the neutral stance, is the most traditional and the one most often taught to beginners. As the ball comes to your forehand side, move into a position so that your feet and shoulders are more or less parallel to the singles sideline. A right-handed player's left shoulder will point toward the net or the ball; a left-handed player's right shoulder will point. In other words, your entire body—upper body, trunk, and lower body—is perpendicular to the net. The main advantage of the square stance is that it allows the hitter to transfer weight forward with the shot. The disadvantage: It takes time to set up perfectly, and time is not always available in rapid exchanges. It's also harder to disguise where you are going with the ball. Smart players may be able to look at your feet and know what you can and cannot do.

Assume the square stance position again. Now move the front foot another step toward the sideline. Instead of your feet forming an imaginary line parallel to the sideline, you have crossed over the line with your front foot. This position is the *closed stance* (figure 1.14). You have no choice but to use this position when you are hitting on the run or playing certain shots. The problem is transfer of weight. When you step across instead of forward, it's virtually impossible to shift your weight in the direction you want to hit. Without a forward weight shift or rotation of the hips, any power you generate has to come from someplace else. It's a mistake to learn the closed stance as the standard for a beginner's forehand; but it is important to know what it is, when to use it, and why you're hitting in that position.

Figure 1.14 Closed stance.

Once again, go back to the square stance. This time instead of stepping closer to the sideline with the front foot, move the front foot slightly to the left and back a bit. This positioning opens your hips and shoulders more toward the net, placing you in the *semiopen stance* (figure 1.15). Although you're giving up some of the forward weight-transfer capacity, you can still generate power. The real advantage of the semiopen stance is that it gives you court coverage options

Figure 1.13 Square stance.

Figure 1.16 Open stance.

Figure 1.15 Semiopen stance.

the square and closed stances don't offer. The position of the left foot allows you to hit and get a head start in recovering and moving to cover the open court. A quick recovery may not seem like a big deal, but saving a split second or a half step can mean the difference between winning and losing points. The semiopen stance is used by elite-level players extensively, especially those players who are baseline specialists. The combination of a semiwestern grip and a semiopen stance allows a player to swing hard and hit hard—a very appealing way to play the game. Be aware of the seimiopen stance, experiment with it, and use it if it's a good fit. Some teachers prefer to teach the semiopen as the stance of choice for beginning players; most instructors, however, still start players with the square stance.

Once more, use the square stance as a starting point. Now move to the semiopen stance, but don't stop there. Go all the way to an *open stance*, in which your feet and shoulders are parallel to the baseline and the net (figure 1.16). You can even use the ready position as a guide to where your feet should be. Your feet are already in the correct position. Everything—shoulders, hips, and feet—is open to the net. In the open stance, a player swings without trying to line the feet up with anything. When the weight shifts in

the open stance, the shift is to the outside foot. Power is generated by an explosive arm action and by rotating the hips with, not before, the swing. Many tournament players use the open stance effectively with a semiwestern or western grip. They can hit hard, disguise the direction of their shots, and be in a great position to cover the court after a hit. The open stance is a good option when you don't have time to set up in another stance, when the ball comes at you directly, and when you have to move wide to hit a forehand.

The open-versus-square stance debate among tennis players has been ongoing for decades. The arguments usually have fallen along age-group lines. Older players believe in the traditional stance (shoulders and feet parallel to the sidelines), whereas younger players and their teachers prefer a shoulders-parallel-to-the-net style.

The arguments are simple enough. The square stance allows for a coordinated movement toward the target, a longer hitting zone, and greater racket speed. The advantage of the open stance is quicker recovery and better court coverage.

Finally, someone has reviewed the limited amount of research on this subject, conducted his own investigation, and drawn some conclusions. Duane Knudson, PhD, a teacher and researcher at California State University in Chico and a member of the USTA Sport Science Committee, concludes that the choice of stances depends on playing ability, physical condition, type of equipment, and match circumstances. Here are some of Knudson's findings:

- The open stance is successful because lighter and stronger rackets and more resilient strings compensate for the shorter swings used by many young players.

- An open stance results in a 4 to 8 percent slower racket-head speed.

- An open stance provides a 4 percent faster recovery than a square stance.

- An open stance and the accompanying racket pathway, which changes by as little as 8 degrees in an upward direction, reduce the margin of error by 60 percent.

- The open stance does not, as previously thought, force players to overuse the trunk and arm.

- The open stance places loads on the shoulder and elbow comparable to those observed in pitching a baseball (and appropriate training methods should be developed).

- Both open and square stances require a large amount of back-muscle activity, which should be taken into account during strength training.

- Intermediate-level players (National Tennis Rating Program [NTRP] skill level of 3.5 to 4.5) can use the open stance, but they are much more likely to mishit the ball.

- Advanced players should use closed-stance forehands in most situations, but they should be able to hit with an open stance when rapid court coverage is required. This conclusion is not consistent with the open-stance approach used by many of the elite players in the world.

Reading about the way to hold a racket and move your feet takes a lot more time than doing it. Everything happens in a hurry during an exchange, so don't get discouraged by wordy explanations. You'll quickly reach a point in your training where you do things without thinking about them first.

Stance and Footwork Drill. Footwork Scramble

Stand at the middle of the service line. Have a partner sit directly behind the net on the opposite side and toss 10 balls anywhere inside the two service courts (figure 1.17). Every time you hit, the partner tosses another ball to a different area of the forecourt. Don't hit hard, and don't worry about forehand or backhand technique. Just concentrate on footwork, using any of the stances described.

For variety, have a partner stand at the net with a basket of balls and toss or hit 10 consecutive balls to your forehand side or down the middle of the court. Return each ball with a forehand to the opposite singles court. Increase difficulty, decrease difficulty, check your fundamentals, and score your success the same as in the original footwork scramble drill. Again, concentrate on footwork, not on stroke production.

To Increase Difficulty

- Hit every shot with a forehand regardless of where it is tossed.

To Decrease Difficulty

- Have your partner feed balls only from the center service line to the singles sideline.

Success Check

- Use shuffle steps for close balls.
- Take crossover steps for balls that are farther away.
- Plant the outside foot to push off in the opposite direction.

Score Your Success

1 to 3 balls returned into the singles court = 3 points

4 to 7 balls returned into the singles court = 5 points

8 to 10 balls returned into the singles court = 7 points

Your score ___

Figure 1.17   Footwork scramble.

BACKSWING

Beginners can simplify the backswing by taking the racket straight back before bringing it straight forward to hit, sort of like a door opening and closing. Very quickly, however, players develop their own unique backswing styles. As long as you stay within some general guidelines, it's okay to develop your own style of backswing.

The first rule is to start getting the racket ready (and turning your shoulders) as soon as you know where the ball is going. Don't wait for the bounce on your side. The second rule is to find a backswing position that is neither too short nor too long. Beginners can start by taking the racket back far enough to point it toward the back fence or wall. More experienced players may take the racket back farther in certain situations. If your backswing is short, you can't hit with power. If the backswing is too long, however, the margin of error increases. Besides, you don't always have time for a long backswing. The last rule is to develop an abbreviated looping motion with your racket—up, back, then a slight hesitation before swinging forward to hit the ball. A diagram of the loop would look similar to a backward letter C.

FORWARD SWING

Now you're ready to hit something. Every drill up to this point has been done to get into a solid hitting position and to build, in segments, momentum for the forward swing. The forward swing is a chain reaction of separate events that starts with your feet on the way to contact. Taking a horizontal swing path with the racket face perpendicular to the court is sufficient for beginners. Even world-class players flatten the trajectories of their swings when they want to hit hard and flat.

Otherwise, the swing is forward and upward, brushing the back of the ball (figure 1.18). The more vertical the swing path, the more topspin is put on the ball. Topspin is good for control, consistency, and for making the ball bounce high on the other side.

Keep your head still, hold the racket with a firm grip, and make contact early. Wrist action is more significant in today's strokes than in the past. Whereas the traditional eastern forehand grip requires a relatively fixed wrist position for most

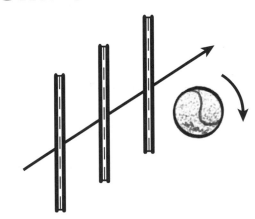

Figure 1.18 Swing path for topspin.

shots, players who use a western or semiwestern grip put a lot of stress on the wrist and forearm as they whip up and across the back of the ball. Try to make contact before the ball reaches a point even with the midsection of your body. Some teachers say to hit the ball a foot in front of the body. You can't always hit that far out, but do try.

15

Forward-Swing Drill 1. *Toss to Forehand*

Stand behind the service line in the middle of the court, and have your practice partner toss 10 consecutive balls so that they bounce waist high to your forehand. Your objective is to return with a forehand inside the singles court (figure 1.19).

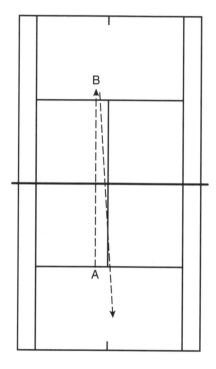

Figure 1.19 Toss to forehand.

To Increase Difficulty

- Start the drill from the baseline.
- Have your partner increase the pace of setups.
- Have your partner hit, rather than toss, setups.

To Decrease Difficulty

- Reduce the pace of setups.
- Start with the racket back.

Success Check

- Focus on control, not power.
- Use a horizontal or down-to-up swing.

Score Your Success

1 to 3 successful forehands = 3 points

4 to 7 successful forehands = 5 points

7 to 10 successful forehands = 7 points

Your score ___

Forward-Swing Drill 2. *Drop-and-Hit Forehands*

This drill will help you get used to hitting in front. From the baseline, assume a square stance with the racket ready for its miniloop. Drop 10 consecutive balls in front and to the side of where you are standing. Strike the ball at a point approximately even with the front foot. After the bounce, hit each ball at a safe height over the net and as far into the backcourt as possible. Attempt to put each shot into the opposite singles court. This drill is also the way to begin groundstroke exchanges during practice and warm-ups.

To Increase Difficulty

- Count only those shots that bounce in the opposite backcourt.

To Decrease Difficulty

- Move closer to the net to hit.

Success Check

- Shift your weight in the swing from back to forward.
- Make contact even with the front foot.

Score Your Success

1 to 3 shots in = 1 point

4 to 7 shots in = 3 points

8 to 10 shots in = 5 points

Your score ___

FOLLOW-THROUGH

How you finish a stroke depends on which stance and which grip you use. Semiwestern grips are associated with follow-throughs that wrap around the front of the body, even the neck. The western grip follow-through is shorter and lower, similar to a windshield-wiper motion (figure 1.20). For the eastern grip, the follow-through ends with the racket pointing toward the net (figure 1.21).

All three follow-through methods ensure that you don't slow your swing down before making impact with the ball. Instructors often will say, "Hit through the ball." When you do that, you're allowing for a normal slowdown of the racket

Figure 1.21 Eastern grip follow-through.

head. If you stop short, you'll probably hit the ball short and without much power. You may also expose yourself to the risk of arm and shoulder injuries.

To check your follow-through, have your partner set you up with waist-high forehands. After each stroke, freeze at the end of your follow-through. Check the position of your racket against the guidelines for the follow-through just described.

Figure 1.20 Western grip follow-through.

Follow-Through Drill 1. *Consecutive Forehands*

Start the drill against a partner. Each player is on his or her baseline. Either player drops and puts a ball into play to the forehand side of the opposite court (figure 1.22). Count the number of total consecutive forehands hit by both players working as a team.

One variation of the consecutive forehands drill is the consecutive crosscourt forehands drill (figure 1.23). Execute the same drill, but hit all forehands crosscourt (forehand to forehand). Balls that do not fall into the opposing crosscourt singles area are misses. To make this variation even more interesting, put an empty tennis ball can on the handle of a squeegee and lean it against the net at the center (figure 1.24). Try to

hit each crosscourt forehand high enough to clear the squeegee without going out.

A second variation is the wall-ball forehands drill (figure 1.25). Stand 20 feet from a practice wall. Try to keep the ball in play against the wall with softly hit forehands. The idea is to control the ball, not to hit the ball hard.

Finally, try the alleys-only variation (figure 1.26). Stand opposite your practice partner at the baseline behind the doubles alley. Keep the ball in play with forehands and try to make all shots bounce in the opposite alley. This variation is very difficult and is better suited for intermediate and advanced players.

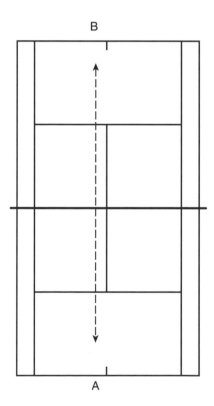

Figure 1.22 Consecutive forehands.

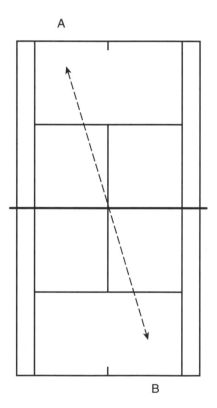

Figure 1.23 Consecutive crosscourt forehands.

Figure 1.24 Clear the squeegee.

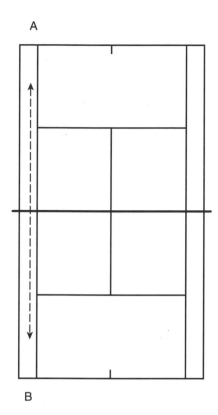

A

B

Figure 1.26 Alleys only.

Figure 1.25 Wall-ball forehands.

To Increase Difficulty

- Each player has to hit up to 10 consecutive forehands (20 total shots).

To Decrease Difficulty

- When one player misses a shot, put another ball in play and continue the count for the player who has not made a mistake.
- Conduct the drill from the service lines instead of the baselines.

Success Check

- Prepare early.
- Make contact in front.
- Complete your follow-through.

Score Your Success

1 to 3 consecutive forehands = 3 points

4 to 7 consecutive forehands = 5 points

8 to 10 consecutive forehands = 7 points

Your score ___

Follow-Through Drill 2.   *Forehand Games*

This drill is the final test of your forehand. From the baseline, put 10 balls into play against a partner's forehand on the opposite baseline. After the setup and return, play the point out. Every stroke has to be hit to your opponent's forehand and with your forehand. Go for winners when you can.

To Increase Difficulty

- Play every shot with a forehand even if the ball goes to your backhand side.

To Decrease Difficulty

- Keep the ball in play rather than trying to hit winners.

Success Check

- Move the feet quickly.
- Prepare the racket early.
- Keep your wrist laid back.
- Make contact in front.

Score Your Success

1 to 3 points won = 5 points

4 to 7 points won = 7 points

8 to 10 points won = 9 points

Your score ___

SUCCESS SUMMARY

Great players make tennis look easy because while we're watching the ball on one side of the court, they are already getting ready for the next shot on their side. For great forehands, stay busy with your feet. Use a shuffle or crossover step to move quickly to get into position, whether your stance is open, closed, semiopen, or square. Turn the shoulders, take the racket back, and use an abbreviated loop before hitting all the way through the ball. Make contact even with the front foot. Expect every shot to come back.

As soon as you've hit a forehand—just like the great players do—use your off hand to adjust your grip and start getting into position for the next shot.

Go back and look at the numbers you recorded in the Score Your Success section for each drill. Enter your scores in table 1.1, and add them to rate your forehand success. If you scored at least 24 out of 50 possible points, go to step 2, the backhand.

Table 1.1   Scoring Summary

Footwork Drills	
1. Grounders	_____ out of 5
2. One-bounce catch	_____ out of 5
3. Shuffle-crossover step	_____ out of 5
Stance and Footwork Drill	
1. Footwork scramble	_____ out of 7
Forward-Swing Drills	
1. Toss to forehand	_____ out of 7
2. Drop-and-hit forehands	_____ out of 5
Follow-Through Drills	
1. Consecutive forehands	_____ out of 7
2. Forehand games	_____ out of 9
TOTAL	_____ ***out of 50***

Turning the Backhand Into a Strength

There is no getting around it—the backhand is a challenge. That is why one of the most common bits of advice coaches give their players is, "Play his backhand," or "Serve to her backhand." The backhand is not a very natural stroke compared to the forehand. For many players, the backhand is weaker. It is a stroke that can be difficult to learn. The backhand requires a certain degree of strength, a grip change, solid footwork, and reliable stroke mechanics.

In spite of these negatives, you can develop a backhand that, like your forehand, becomes an offensive weapon instead of a defensive liability. Your goal is for opponents and their coaches to say instead, "Stay away from his backhand," or "Don't serve to her backhand."

There are more ways to hold and swing the racket on a backhand than on a forehand. If you are new to tennis, you'll have to experiment with two or three grips and swing patterns to find the ones most comfortable for your body and your style of play. If you've been playing for a while, it might be time to see if a slight grip change can make your backhand better.

Most players are satisfied if they simply develop a backhand that won't get them into trouble. As they get better, they begin to realize that the backhand can be just as effective for winning points as the forehand. Once you have a competent backhand, think in terms of building points on both sides, forehand and backhand. Develop winning groundstroke patterns. Make the other player expect a certain shot placement, then hit it to another part of the court. Use backhand and forehand combinations to make your opponent cover a lot of ground on the other side. When you are in position for a winning forehand, backhand, volley, or any other shot, go for it. Specific suggestions for backhand tactics appear in steps 9 and 10.

Several of the footwork and forehand drills in step 1 can also be effective on the backhand side. Step 1 drills that apply equally to backhand practice include grounders, one-bounce catch, shuffle-crossover step, and footwork scramble. Tips for increasing and decreasing difficulty, checking your success, and scoring your success are the same as those in step 1.

ONE-HANDED BACKHAND

The traditional grip for the one-handed backhand is the eastern backhand grip. In the eastern backhand grip, a right-handed player's wrist should be slightly to the left of the top of the racket handle when looking down on the racket, with the racket's edges perpendicular to the court (figure 2.1a). A left-handed player's wrist will be slightly to the right of the top (figure 2.1b). Think of your thumb as having a top, bottom, outside, and inside. The inside part of the thumb should be in contact with the back flat bevel of the racket handle. You can align your thumb in different positions along that part of the grip, but it is essential that the inside part be in contact with the racket. During a point, the thumb's position may change, but the part of the thumb that touches the grip should not.

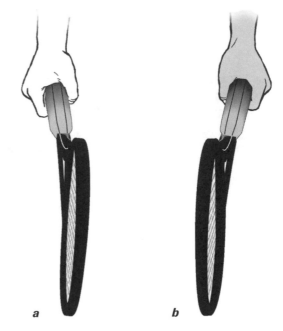

Figure 2.2 Continental backhand grip: *(a)* right-handed player; *(b)* left-handed player.

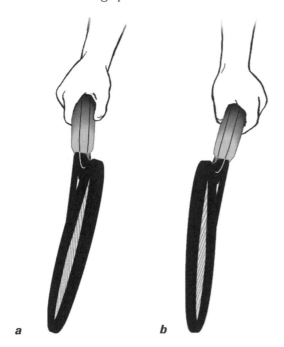

Figure 2.1 Eastern backhand grip: *(a)* right-handed player; *(b)* left-handed player.

You can experiment with the continental grip (figure 2.2), but unless you have a very strong forearm the grip won't work. With a continental grip, the wrist is directly on top of the racket handle. The thumb has to provide more support from the rear because the wrist is not positioned behind the racket. Extend your thumb along the back of the grip so that the inside part is in

contact and pushing against the racket handle during the stroke. If you use a continental grip for the forehand (few players do), you won't have to change grips to hit a backhand. The disadvantage is that some players feel uncomfortable hitting shots this way on either side of the body because the continental grip is halfway between the conventional eastern forehand and backhand grips.

Regardless of how you hold the racket, start turning your shoulders and taking the racket back as soon as the ball leaves the other player's racket. Learn to prepare as you move to hit; don't wait until the last second. Use your off hand to cradle the racket at the throat or shaft. Leave that hand on the racket throat during the entire backswing and use it to adjust your grip after hitting every shot.

When hitting the one-handed backhand (figure 2.3), beginning players should bring the racket back in a line horizontal to the court at about waist height. Think of drawing a sword out of your pocket. More advanced players can try to develop a small loop by bringing the racket back higher than the waist, then dropping down before swinging forward.

Figure 2.3 One-Handed Backhand

a   b   c

PREPARATION

1. Eastern grip
2. Cradle racket at throat with opposite hand
3. Racket back early
4. Early shoulder turn
5. Square stance when time permits

SWING

1. Shift weight forward
2. Parallel or low-to-high swing path
3. Make contact early

FOLLOW-THROUGH

1. Out
2. Across
3. Up

Three of the stance options for the forehand are also options for the backhand. The closed stance is a necessity on some shots, but it is not recommended as the setup of choice. The semiopen stance is good for court coverage, but players using this stance may find it a little difficult to generate power. The ideal stance for the backhand is the square stance because it is good for transferring weight forward. A completely open stance is not an option for the one-handed backhand. Although the open stance is great for covering the court, it is only useful to players who use a two-handed backhand. Whatever stance you choose, be sure to spread your feet comfortably to establish a wide base of support.

Beginning players should swing in a trajectory approximately parallel to the court. Concentrate on taking the racket back in a straight line and bringing it forward in a straight line. You can get fancy with the backhand as you develop your game. Intermediate players should bring the racket back a little higher than the waist and then drop it down before swinging forward and upward through an imaginary tunnel. The body rotates into the shot, although the rotation is greater in the upper body and shoulders than it is in the hips. Visualize the path of the backswing–forward swing as a walking cane positioned not parallel but instead tilted slightly up at the bottom pointing toward the ball. A little hook at the back represents the miniloop backswing; the swing then continues in a straight line going up to the ball. The racket face ought to be perpendicular to the court on contact.

Keep your wrist firmly in place and cocked up throughout the swing. The racket head should be higher than your wrist on all but very low shots. Try to make contact with the ball when it is even with or in front of the front foot. Extend your arm comfortably when you swing. Find a comfort zone, and groove your swing through that zone in a consistent manner.

Follow through with the swing out toward the net, across the front of your body, and up, in that order. Think of reaching out for the net with the back of your hand, then bringing the racket up and across. Finish the stroke by pointing generally in the direction of the target.

TWO-HANDED BACKHAND

Hitting a backhand with two hands on the handle is as common, if not more so, than the one-handed backhand. The two-handed backhand (figure 2.4) adds power, helps control the swing, and provides a better racket position to hit the ball with topspin. The two-handed backhand, however, is not for everyone. The disadvantages of this option include not being able to reach as far for wide shots, an inability to maneuver the racket easily on shots hit directly at the player, and the lack of strength development in the dominant arm.

| Figure 2.4 | Two-Handed Backhand |

a   b   c

PREPARATION
1. Two eastern forehand grips, one eastern backhand grip combined with an eastern forehand, or a continental grip–eastern grip combination
2. Quick upper-body turn
3. Open, semiopen, or square stance

SWING
1. Low-to-high swing path
2. Lift with the legs, but keep head down
3. Uncoil body with the swing
4. Contact even with or slightly past center of body

FOLLOW-THROUGH
1. Up
2. Across

The two-handed backhand can be held in several ways. The simplest is to use an eastern forehand grip with the strong hand and add an eastern forehand grip with the other hand (figure 2.5). The hands touch each other, and the fingers are spread along the racket grip. Some players prefer to use an eastern backhand grip with the strong hand and an eastern forehand grip with the other hand, whereas others use a continental grip–eastern grip combination.

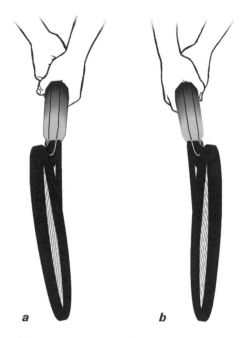

Figure 2.5 Two-handed backhand grip using two eastern forehand grips: *(a)* right-handed player; *(b)* left-handed player.

Countless other grip combinations involving both hands can be used, but try not to get confused. If you use one hand to hit the backhand, make your first choice an eastern forehand grip and support the racket on the throat with the opposite hand. If you use two hands, try using a continental or eastern backhand grip with the dominant hand. The second hand should take an eastern or semiwestern forehand grip. From that starting point you can experiment with slight changes and find the combination that is right for you.

Use the dominant hand to make whatever grip change is needed quickly, and add your choice of grips with the other hand. While you're getting the right grip and turning your shoulders, you should be moving toward the ball and getting ready to plant your feet. Bring the racket back into a lower position before driving up and forward to hit the ball with topspin. Put backspin on the ball by starting with the racket a bit higher than the waist and using an up-to-down swing path. Turn your hips and shoulders, even to the point of showing your back to your opponent. Be ready to uncoil your body into the swing.

A closed stance is not a good position for hitting a two-handed backhand. Depending on the circumstances, position your feet to hit from a square stance, a semiopen stance (for a combination of power and court coverage), or an open stance (figure 2.6). Form a strong base of support by spreading your feet wider than

Figure 2.6 Stances for the two-handed backhand: *(a)* square, *(b)* semiopen, *(c)* open.

27

your shoulders. Players who use the two-handed backhand rely on the completely open stance to uncoil their bodies into the shot and to get a head start on recovering for the next return. Right-handed players bring the left foot around to the side with or after the swing to push off in the opposite direction. Left-handed players do the same with the right foot.

The wrist action is more significant if you hit the backhand with two hands. Bring the racket through the ball with a down-to-up motion. Your arms will be closer to your body than in a one-handed backhand. Players who hit effective two-handed backhands uncoil their bodies into the shot starting with the hips. One of the advantages of the two-handed backhand is that you can wait longer to make contact. Contact doesn't have to happen out in front. The follow-through will whip across the front of your body and may even wrap around your neck.

Backhand Drill 1. *Toss to Backhand*

This drill is a good one to use to get the feel of the backswing, whether one-handed or two-handed. Stand behind the service line in the middle of the court and have your partner toss 10 consecutive balls so they bounce waist-high to your backhand (figure 2.7). The objective is to hit a return that lands inside the singles court.

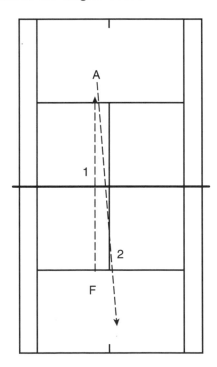

Figure 2.7 Toss to backhand.

To Increase Difficulty

- Start the drill from the baseline.
- Have your partner increase the pace of setups.
- Have your partner hit, rather than toss, setups.

To Decrease Difficulty

- Reduce the pace of setups.
- Practice drop-and-hit backhands, but have a partner drop the ball on your backhand side.

Success Check

- Focus on control, not power.
- Use a horizontal or down-to-up swing.

Score Your Success

1 to 3 successful backhands = 3 points

4 to 7 successful backhands = 5 points

7 to 10 successful backhands = 7 points

Your score ___

Backhand Drill 2. *Consecutive Backhands*

Consecutive backhands offers another way to get used to holding and swinging the racket for a backhand stroke. Stand on or just behind the service line. Drop and softly put a ball into play to your partner's backhand (figure 2.8). Count the number of consecutive soft-hit backhands, or bumps, you can hit before making an error.

This drill has a couple of fun variations as well. For the consecutive baseline backhand variation,

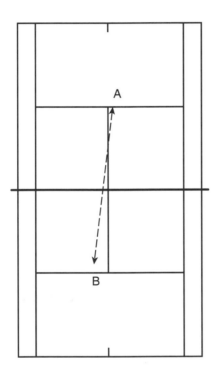

Figure 2.8 Consecutive backhands.

instead of playing from the service line, move back to your respective baselines and count the number of consecutive backhands exchanged. For the alleys-only variation, you and your practice partner stand on opposite ends of the court behind the doubles alley. Keep the ball in play with backhands, trying to make all shots bounce in the opposite alley.

To Increase Difficulty

- Start the drill three steps behind the service line.
- Start the drill from the baseline (see variation 1).

To Decrease Difficulty

- Pick up the count after every missed shot instead of starting over.

Success Check

- Place the off hand on the racket throat.
- Rotate the shoulders quickly.

Score Your Success

1 to 3 consecutive backhand bumps = 3 points

4 to 7 consecutive backhand bumps = 5 points

8 to 10 consecutive backhand bumps = 7 points

Your score ____

Backhand Drill 3. *Backhand Games*

From the baseline, put 10 balls into play to a partner's backhand on the opposite baseline. After the setup and return, play the point out. Every stroke has to be hit to your opponent's backhand and with your backhand. Restart the point when shots are not hit to a reasonable backhand position. Go for winners when you can.

To Increase Difficulty

- Play every shot with a backhand even if the ball goes to your forehand side.

To Decrease Difficulty

- Keep the ball in play rather than trying to hit winners.

Success Check

- Move the feet quickly.
- Prepare the racket early.
- Complete your follow-through.

Score Your Success

1 to 3 points won = 5 points

4 to 7 points won = 7 points

8 to 10 points won = 9 points

Your score ___

Backhand Drill 4. *Two-Minute Drill*

Now it's time to combine forehand and backhand groundstrokes. Start the two-minute drill at the baseline. Return balls tossed randomly to your forehand and backhand sides nonstop for a period of two minutes. Count the number of in shots in segments of 10 attempts. Restart the count after 10 shots, but continue the drill for two minutes.

To Increase Difficulty

- Return every shot with a forehand (or every shot with a backhand), regardless of where it's tossed.
- Return every shot to the backhand side of your practice partner.
- Have your partner hit, rather than toss, setups.

To Decrease Difficulty

- Have your partner alternately toss to your forehand and backhand.
- Have your partner toss to the same side with every ball.

Success Check

- Don't watch to see where your shots go.
- Shorten your swing when in trouble.
- Practice a "get-to-everything" attitude.

Score Your Success

1 to 3 successful groundstrokes in any 10-shot sequence = 5 points

4 to 7 successful groundstrokes = 7 points

8 to 10 successful groundstrokes = 9 points

Your score ___

Backhand Drill 5. *Groundstroke Games*

To test your groundstrokes in a competitive situation, drill with groundstroke games. From the baseline, either player puts 10 balls into play anywhere in the opposite backcourt. After the setup and return, play the point out hitting forehands and backhands. Go for winners when you can.

To Increase Difficulty

- Exchange four consecutive groundstrokes before scoring begins.
- Score a point only when you force your opponent into making an error.

To Decrease Difficulty

- Score 2 points when you force your opponent to make an error.

Success Check

- After each shot, recover to a point midway between the angles of possible return.
- Make contact early on forehands.
- Build points to get into a winning situation.

Score Your Success

1 to 3 points won = 5 points

4 to 7 points won = 7 points

8 to 10 points won = 9 points

Your score ____

ALTERED GROUNDSTROKES: RETURNING THE SERVE

If your opponent is serving from the deuce court, stand on the right side of the court as you face the net on or slightly behind the baseline, near the singles sideline (figure 2.9*a*). When your opponent serves from the ad court, stand along the baseline on your court's left side near the opposite singles sideline (figure 2.9*b*).

As in returning any other shot in tennis, the idea is to position yourself in the middle of extreme angles to which your opponent can serve. If your opponent has a weak first serve or a second serve with less pace, move forward a step or two before the serve. Against a fast serve, especially on a fast court, play deeper to give yourself more time to react.

A beginning player will serve weakly, so return the serve just as you would return any other groundstroke. Watch your opponent's racket face as he or she hits the serve. As soon as you determine whether the ball is coming to your forehand or backhand, adjust grips. If you are already holding a forehand grip and the serve comes to the forehand side, no adjustment is

necessary. If the serve comes to the other side, however, change to either the eastern or two-handed backhand grip.

Move to the ball while turning your shoulders and getting your racket back early. If you have time, step forward and swing in a parallel-to-the-court or slightly upward motion. Play the ball, not your opponent. Concentrate on the service return as if you were returning forehands or backhands in a groundstroke drill. The idea is to put the ball in play and begin getting into a position to win the point. If you can control the ball, think crosscourt, high over the net, and deep into your opponent's backcourt.

Returning an advanced serve presents a new combination of problems. The ball comes faster than a groundstroke or a beginner's serve, leaving less time to prepare. Be extra alert to return a hard-hit serve. Get into the ready position, racket forward, on your toes, and leaning forward. Many players take a short hop just as their opponent strikes the ball. This movement puts their bodies into motion for a quick reaction.

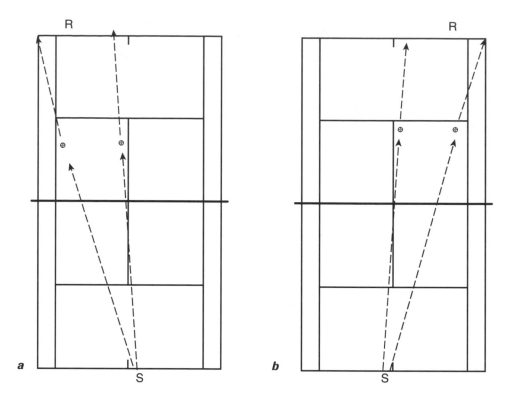

Figure 2.9 Returning the serve: *(a)* from the deuce court; *(b)* from the ad court.

You may not have time to set up in a traditional square stance to transfer your weight forward. Turn your shoulders and shorten your backswing. Insufficient time also may not allow you to take a full, looping swing like many players use to return groundstrokes. If you have time, however, go ahead and step forward quickly with the opposite foot.

Finally, do not fight power with power. If your opponent serves hard, hold your racket tightly and block the shot (return the ball with a very short swinging motion). Use the pace provided by the serve. If the ball comes at a slower pace, then you can go back to your normal preparation and supply the power yourself.

SUCCESS SUMMARY

At most skill levels, the player who can keep the ball in play four or five times during a point will win. The immediate goal for the backhand is consistency. Once you can put the backhand where you want it consistently, start working on power. The keys are quick footwork and upper-body rotation during preparation and a smooth but strong swing all the way through the ball. Experiment with a variety of one-handed and two-handed grips and decide which one is right for you. Find a groove so you don't even have to think about the mechanics of hitting the shot. Make contact early. In your mind, determine that nothing your opponent hits can get past you.

Enter the numbers you recorded for each drill in table 2.1. Add them to rate your backhand success. If you scored at least 20 out of 41 possible points, move to step 3 to learn the serve.

Table 2.1   Scoring Summary

Backhand Drills	
1. Toss to backhand	_____ out of 7
2. Consecutive backhands	_____ out of 7
3. Backhand games	_____ out of 9
4. Two-minute drill	_____ out of 9
5. Groundstroke games	_____ out of 9
TOTAL	_____ *out of 41*

Serving to Set Up Points

Every stroke in tennis except one, the serve, is influenced by how, when, and where your opponent hits the ball. The serve, however, is all up to you. A strong serve (not necessarily a hard serve) means you can immediately start setting up the point to your advantage. A weak or inconsistent serve means your opponent takes that advantage away. Accept credit for a good serving game, and don't blame anyone else if you have a poor serve. It's your responsibility to serve well; doing so is completely under your control.

The importance of the serve is reflected in the phrases *hold serve* and *break serve*. You are expected to hold serve—to win games in which you are the server—because you are getting a free shot at your opponent to start the point. Hold every serve and you can't lose unless the match goes into a tiebreaker. Hold serve every time and break one serve of your opponent, and you win the set.

For both beginner and intermediate players, the strategy for the serve is simple: Do everything you can to hold it. Getting at least 60 percent of first serves in sets the stage for winning games. Serve down the middle to take advantage of a lower net and reduce the angle of your opponent's return. Serve to the backhand side if your opponent has a weak backhand. Serve deep to keep your opponent from attacking your serve. Serve wide to either side to open up the court for your next shot. For tactics in specific situations and against certain kinds of opponents, read steps 9 through 11.

It's harder for beginners to hold serve because they haven't had enough time to develop the serve into an offensive tool. The objectives for beginners learning the serve are to work on technique, strength, and consistency. But at the intermediate and advanced levels of tennis, the serve becomes the first bullet fired. The following explanations, illustrations, and drills will help you develop a serve, beginning with the punch serve for beginners and continuing to an intermediate and advanced full-swing serve that can be used at any level of the game. Intermediate and advanced players may decide to skip the punch-serve section.

SERVICE ROUTINE

Good servers go through the same routine before each serve. The routine may involve bouncing the ball a couple of times, taking a deep breath, looking at the target area, positioning the feet in a certain way, or all of the above.

"Routines provide anchors for athletes," says Keith Henschen, PhD, professor in the department of exercise and sports science at the University of Utah. "There is a certain amount of security in knowing what is about to happen. This knowledge helps athletes prepare for competition in a way that makes them feel most secure. For some, the routine is a crutch. For others, it just serves to get them where they want to be. But for all athletes, the luxury of having a routine is a positive way to enhance performance."

Routines can be classified as long term, game day, and in the moment. Each routine has a different purpose. "Long-term routines are patterns of behavior that athletes follow for at least five to six days before an event," explains Henschen, who has worked with amateur and professional athletes. "It includes sleeping, eating, and training schedules that keep things on an even keel so that there are no events that disrupt the athlete's life. This is easier for the professional athlete to control than for those of us who have equally important obligations that are not sports related."

Game-day routines take a sharper focus on issues such as what time to get up, when and what to eat, where to be at given times during the day, and what potential distractions may arise so they can be avoided. For tennis players, the game-day routine almost always includes a hitting session well before the prematch warm-up.

The last type of routine is the in-the-moment routine. Henschen explains that the purpose of having a series of in-the-moment routines is twofold. First, this routine increases the arousal level needed to perform; second and almost paradoxically, it lowers anxiety. The idea is to get to the optimal zone of performance. This is where the pre-serve routine comes into play.

You may have already developed a routine of which you are not even aware. Get a friend or coach to observe what you do before each serve. It is not uncommon for inexperienced players to do something different every time. Beginners are, in effect, reinventing the wheel over and over again.

"Don't confuse routines with rituals," warns Henschen. "Rituals have more to do with superstition (like former major league baseball player Wade Boggs, who ate chicken before each game for 15 years). Routines are not as emotionally based as rituals. If you miss part of a routine, you can compensate for it. Athletes who are locked into rituals think they can't perform well if their rituals are not completed. Routines are about comfort; rituals can cause discomfort." Henschen's message for tennis players: "Routines at all three levels are good. Follow them if they work. But don't rely on rituals. Then you start depending on them to perform well instead of trusting yourself."

Step 3 begins with the punch serve for beginners, but those of you who are intermediate players can skip this section and go right to the full-swing serve. Whatever your level, the first objective is to get your serve into play consistently while using the proper technique. When you can do that almost automatically, the next goal is to be able to place the ball wherever you want it to go within the opponent's service court. The third objective is to hit increasingly more powerful serves, and the last objective is to be able to hit with a variety of spins. Once you can get serves into the service court, to a specific area of that court, with power, and with spin, you're no longer a beginner or an intermediate server. Now, you're an advanced player—at least when you put the ball into play with a serve.

PUNCH SERVE

For the punch serve (figure 3.1), hold the racket with an eastern forehand grip. As your serving motion becomes more fluid, change your grip to a continental or modified continental.

Stand behind the baseline at about a 45-degree angle to the net, facing one of the net posts. If you are right-handed, position your left foot forward at a 45-degree angle; if you are

| Figure 3.1 | **Punch Serve** |

 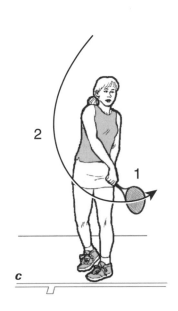

PREPARATION

1. Eastern forehand grip
2. Stand facing net post
3. Tossing arm extended forward
4. Racket behind head
5. Toss up and forward

SWING

1. Lean forward
2. Reach high to hit

FOLLOW-THROUGH

1. Continue swing after hit
2. Out, across, down

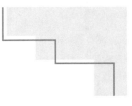

Misstep

The serve is short.

Correction

Don't let the ball drop too low during the toss.

Misstep

The serve lacks control.

Correction

Increase the number of practice repetitions.

left-handed, position and angle your right foot forward. The foot away from the baseline should be placed so that an imaginary line between the toes of both feet would point in the direction you want to serve. Within reason, the exact alignment of the feet is a matter of individual preference.

To toss the ball, hold the ball at the base of your fingers. Extend your arm, holding the ball in the direction you want to hit, and lift the ball without bending very much at the elbow. As you lift, release the ball by opening your fingers. The ball should go up with little or no spin. Toss the ball so it reaches a peak higher than the tip of the racket. Work on tossing the ball to the same spot consistently. You may not toss the ball perfectly every time, but developing a reliable toss will be one less thing that can go wrong. The service-toss target drill will help you groove the toss.

Toss Drill 1. *Service-Toss Target*

Take a position behind the baseline. Extend your arm and racket up and forward to gauge the proper height. Practice 10 consecutive service tosses (figure 3.2). Let the ball drop to the court. Points accrue when the ball falls inside the baseline.

To Increase Difficulty

- Place a small towel or other target a few inches inside the baseline and count only those tosses that hit the target.

To Decrease Difficulty

- Use a bigger target.

Success Check

- Begin tossing movement in the shoulder joint.
- Extend fingers with the toss.
- Follow the ball with your hand and eyes.

Score Your Success

1 to 3 successful tosses = 1 point

4 to 7 successful tosses = 3 points

8 to 10 successful tosses = 5 points

Your score ___

Figure 3.2 Service-toss target.

Toss Drill 2.   *Ready, Aim, Throw*

Stand at the baseline of one court near the center mark. Attempt to throw 10 consecutive balls diagonally into the opposite service court.

To Increase Difficulty

- Change positions along the baseline with each throw.
- Start from a position one to two steps behind the baseline.

To Decrease Difficulty

- Start from a position one to two steps behind the service line.
- Score a point if the toss lands anywhere in the opposite singles court.

Success Check

- Place opposite shoulder and hip toward the net to start motion.
- Step in the direction of the throw with opposite foot.
- Take the throwing arm down and back, bend it, and extend arm up and forward.
- Reach high to release.

Score Your Success

1 to 3 successful throws = 1 point

4 to 7 successful throws = 3 points

8 to 10 successful throws = 5 points

Your score ___

Bring the racket to a position behind your back and touch the middle of your back with the edge of your racket. Lift the racket head a few inches and make this your starting point. Swing up at the ball. The serve motion goes up before it goes forward. Don't let your elbow lead the stroke; keep it high until after the hit. When you hit, reach as high as you can. Your arm and racket should be fully extended when contact is made. With the hit, snap your wrist.

The swing to serve a tennis ball is not exactly like the throwing motion, but it has many things in common with throwing a baseball or softball. If you can throw well, you can probably serve well. To assess your throwing ability, try the ready, aim, throw drill. After contact, continue to bring the racket forward toward the net as far as it will go. Follow through across the front of your body, ending on the opposite side from which the motion began.

Punch-Serve Drill 1.   *Service-Line Serves*

Put the entire serving motion into action by serving 10 consecutive balls into the proper service court, but serve from a position behind the service line instead of the baseline.

To Increase Difficulty

- Move back to a position halfway between the service line and the baseline.
- Serve five times from the deuce court, five times from the ad court.

To Decrease Difficulty

- Move forward to a position inside the service line.

Success Check

- Start with racket behind head or back.
- Toss higher than you can reach.
- Reach high to hit.
- Keep the head up.

Score Your Success

1 to 3 successful serves = 3 points

4 to 7 successful serves = 5 points

8 to 10 successful serves = 7 points

Your score ___

Punch-Serve Drill 2. *Target Serves*

To practice directing serves deep and to specific spots, place a piece of tape across the service court to divide it into two halves, front and back (figure 3.3). Stand behind the baseline near the center mark and serve 10 consecutive balls into the area between the tape and the service line.

For variety, try long-distance serves. Instead of serving from the baseline position, serve from a position two steps behind the baseline. Another variation of the drill is box targets. Place a large cardboard box or similar target deep and in the middle of the service court. Count the number of times your serve hits the target. Move the targets into the service-court corners to make the drill even more difficult (figure 3.4).

To Increase Difficulty

- Use tape to divide the back service into two areas, and serve alternately into each target area.

To Decrease Difficulty

- Move the tape closer to the net to allow a larger target area.

Success Check

- Aim deep.
- Snap the wrist on contact.

Score Your Success

1 to 3 serves into the target area = 5 points

4 to 7 serves into the target area = 7 points

8 to 10 serves into the target area = 9 points

Your score ___

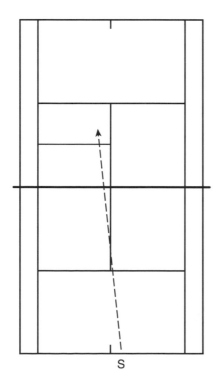

Figure 3.3 Target serves.

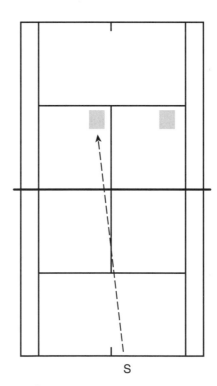

Figure 3.4 Box target serves.

Punch-Serve Drill 3. *Serve and Return Games*

Play a 10-point game with a partner using only the serve and service return. The server earns 1 point for every in serve. The receiver gets a point for every successful return. The server gets two chances to get the ball into play. Change from right to left sides on the baseline after five serves.

To Increase Difficulty

• Allow the server only one chance to put the ball into play.

To Decrease Difficulty

• Serve all 10 attempts from the same position.

Success Check

• Concentrate on your serve, not your opponent's return.
• Make mistakes long, not short.
• Strive for consistency, not power.

Score Your Success

The server earns 3 points for every 1 to 3 successful serves, 5 points for every 4 to 7 successful serves, and 7 points for every 8 to 10 successful serves.

The receiver earns 3 points for every 1 to 3 successful returns, 5 points for every 4 to 7 successful returns, and 7 points for every 8 to 10 successful returns.

Your score ___

FULL-SWING SERVE

Intermediate and advanced players can use the full-swing serve (figure 3.5) to put the ball in play. Rather than just shooting for targets, imagine yourself in game situations in which you are up 40-30 and poised to win a game (or set) with a strong serve, or down 30-40 and in danger of losing a match with a weak serve or double fault.

Figure 3.5   **Full-Swing Serve**

PREPARATION
1. Continental grip
2. Feet at 45-degree angle to net
3. Toss slightly higher than tip of extended racket

a

(continued)

Figure 3.5 *(continued)*

SWING

1. Full down, back, up, and forward motion; some advanced players abbreviate the backswing
2. Full extension with body, arm, and racket to hit
3. Weight shifts forward
4. Wrist snaps and pronates on contact

FOLLOW-THROUGH

1. Out, across, down

Misstep
The serve lacks power.
Correction
Snap (pronate) the wrist on contact with the ball.

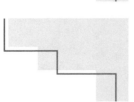

Misstep
The serve goes into the net.
Correction
Keep your head up as you strike the ball.

Hold the racket with a continental grip, although you may want to modify with an eastern forehand to hit the ball flatter or an eastern backhand to create a topspin effect. With the continental grip, the wrist is directly over the top of the racket handle as you look down on it.

Position your feet at a 45-degree angle to the net, spread more than shoulder-width apart. Turn your side to the net so you can rotate, or uncoil, your body into the ball with the swing. The angle at which you stand may vary a few degrees in either direction, depending on individual preference.

To swing, begin with your racket in front of your body, pointing toward the target at about chest height with your free hand holding the ball against the racket strings. Drop your racket head in a pendulum motion so that the racket head passes beside your leg. Some experienced players modify the downswing and backswing, creating an abbreviated motion. Move the ball hand slightly downward before the toss at the same time the racket goes down. Again, some advanced players may delay the tossing or swinging movement to establish their own rhythm, but moving the hands down together then up together is a good starting point. Drop the racket arm down; then move it up into the back-scratching position. Simultaneously, move the other arm up to lift the ball for the toss. The motion should have a rhythmic feel.

Time the toss so that the ball will drop to a point above your head and slightly in front of your body at the same time you extend your racket arm to make contact. If the timing is way off, stop everything and start over. The toss has to be far enough in front of you to force you to lean forward and beyond the baseline as you hit. Keep your head up and look at the ball while you are tossing.

To make the most of the weight transfer, move one foot during the motion. As you lean forward, keep the foot closest to the baseline in the same place, but move your other foot forward. Some players prefer to take one step, starting with the rear foot several inches behind the baseline and finishing one step inside the line. Other players take a two-step approach with the rear foot: Bring the back foot forward to a point just behind the front foot prior to hitting.

This movement results in a springboard effect and may even supply added height and leverage if you get up on your toes to hit.

Whether you employ a one-step or two-step approach with the back foot, be sure to bend your knees while preparing to hit. Part of the uncoiling motion of the body includes exploding upward from a knees-flexed to a knees-extended position. Not only are you turning into the ball, you are also springing up to unleash the chain of events that starts with your feet and continues through the snap of the wrist as you make contact with the ball.

As you bring the racket up and behind your back, your arm should begin to bend at the elbow and move through the back-scratching position. Extend your arm fully to make contact with the ball. When you serve, your body should be almost in a straight line from your toes to your racket hand at the moment of impact. Be sure to snap your wrist on contact with the ball to generate maximum power. The snapping movement of the wrist is called *pronation*, in which the thumb rotates down and away from your body (figure 3.6).

After you hit the ball, continue to move your back foot forward, touching down one step inside the baseline. The follow-through of the arm and racket crosses in front of your body and finishes down on the opposite side.

Figure 3.6 Wrist snap at contact.

Full-Swing Serve Drill 1.   *Consecutive First Serves*

To assess your serve's effectiveness, attempt 10 consecutive first serves. Change from the deuce court to the ad court after the first five serves. Count each successful serve.

To Increase Difficulty

- Alternate serving from deuce and ad positions with every serve.
- Serve only to a right-handed player's backhand side.

To Decrease Difficulty

- Attempt all 10 serves from the same position.

Success Check

- Use a continental grip.
- Toss in front of body higher than extended racket.
- Use a rhythmic serving motion.
- Pronate the wrist on contact.
- Place back foot inside baseline after hit.

Score Your Success

1 to 3 successful serves = 1 point

4 to 7 successful serves = 3 points

8 to 10 successful serves = 5 points

Your score ___

Full-Swing Serve Drill 2.   *Serve and Return Games*

Play a 10-point game with a partner using only the serve and service return. The server gets points for the number of in serves. The receiver gets points for the number of successful returns. The server gets two chances to get the ball into play. Change from right to left sides on the baseline after five serves.

To Increase Difficulty

- Allow the server only one chance to put the ball into play.

To Decrease Difficulty

- Allow the server to stand inside the baseline.

Success Checks

- Concentrate on your serve, not your opponent's return.
- Aim deep.
- Strive for consistency, not power.

Score Your Success

The server earns 3 points for 1 to 3 successful serves, 5 points for 4 to 7 successful serves, and 7 points for 8 to 10 successful serves.

The receiver earns 3 points for 1 to 3 successful returns, 5 points for 4 to 7 successful returns, and 7 points for 8 to 10 successful returns.

Your score ___

Full-Swing Serve Drill 3. *Advanced Target Serves*

To practice directing serves deep and to specific spots, place a piece of tape across the service court to divide it into two halves, front and back. Stand behind the baseline near the center mark, and serve 10 consecutive balls into the area between the tape and the service line.

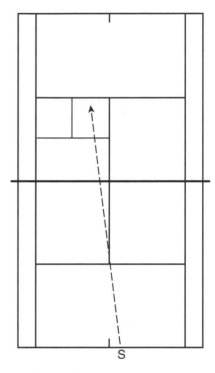

Figure 3.7 Advanced target serves.

To Increase Difficulty

- Use tape to divide the service court into three target areas (forehand corner, backhand corner, and middle; figure 3.7), and serve alternately into each area.

To Decrease Difficulty

- Move the tape closer to the net to allow a larger target area.

Success Check

- Visualize your serve hitting the target area.
- Maintain racket-head speed through the motion.

Score Your Success

1 to 3 serves into the target area = 5 points

4 to 7 serves into the target area = 7 points

8 to 10 serves into the target area = 9 points

Your score ____

SLICE, TOPSPIN, AND FLAT SERVES

The point of contact between the racket and the ball varies depending on the kind of spin you want to put on the ball. For an extreme slice serve, a right-handed player will toss the ball wider to the right than on a conventional serve. The racket strings strike the ball more to the side (at 2:00 or 3:00 instead of 1:00, when imagining the ball as the face of a clock). Think of scooping your racket face around the edge of the ball.

To impart topspin, toss the ball almost directly overhead. The racket brushes upward behind the ball from 7:00 in the direction of 1:00. Contact is farther back than in a normal serving motion. Topspin serves should clear the net by two or three feet. To achieve a topspin effect, change your grip from a continental to an eastern backhand.

Slice and topspin work well on second serves. The racket speed is the same or even faster than on first serves, but the angle at which the racket contacts the ball imparts spin, creating a greater margin of error and a safer service attempt.

To hit a flat, hard serve, some players change from the continental grip to an eastern grip. Instead of trying to put sidespin or topspin on the ball, they position the wrist so the face of the racket strikes the ball flush in the middle of the clock face.

Predictors of a Powerful Serve

Research conducted among tournament-level players at the Johns Hopkins University School of Medicine and reported in the *American Journal of Sports Medicine* identified several factors associated with powerful serves. Following is a summary of the findings. One finding reaffirms the importance of wrist action; one is related to age; and two involve internal rotation, which occurs when the arm is rotated inward toward the body from the shoulder joint.

- The more flexible the wrist, the higher the velocity.
- The older the player, the weaker the serve.
- The greater the flexibility of the shoulder upon moving the arm forward and rotating inward, the more powerful the serve.
- The greater the power exerted with internal rotation, the more powerful the serve.

Serve and Groundstroke Drill 1. *No-Ad Set*

Now that you can hit serves and groundstrokes, it's time to play tennis. Play a set using no-ad scoring. The first player to win 4 points wins the game. If the score in a game is 3-3, the receiver has the option of receiving the serve from either the left or right side. Do the best you can if you have to hit volleys. Volleys are covered next in step 4.

To Increase Difficulty

- Allow your opponent the choice of right or left side on all 3-3 points.
- The server gets only one attempt to put the serve in play.

To Decrease Difficulty

- You choose right or left sides on all 3-3 points.

- You begin serving the set.
- Allow three attempts to get the serve in.

Success Check

- Allow no double faults.
- Aim for 60 percent successful first serves.

Score Your Success

1 to 2 games won = 1 point

3 to 5 games won = 5 points

Win the set = 9 points

Your score ___

Serve and Groundstroke Drill 2. *Regular Set*

Play a set using conventional scoring. Spin the racket in the hands to determine side and first serve. Change ends of the court every time the total number of games is an odd number.

To Increase Difficulty

- Server gets only one attempt on each service point.

To Decrease Difficulty

- Server gets three attempts on each service point.

Success Check

- Concentrate on holding serve.
- Extend fully on service contact.
- Snap wrist at top of swing.

Score Your Success

1 to 2 games won = 1 point

3 to 5 games won = 5 points

Win the set = 9 points

Your score ___

SUCCESS SUMMARY

The fundamentals for both beginner and intermediate serves are remarkably similar. Position the front foot at a 45-degree angle to the net. Toss higher than you can reach. Extend your body, arm, and racket fully to make contact with the ball. To get more power, increase the speed of the racket head. Follow through out, across, and down, in that order.

For beginners, total the points you earned in each of the five drills in table 3.1. If you scored 16 out of 33 possible points, you're ready for the intermediate-level drills.

Intermediate and advanced players should enter the number of points scored in each of the five drills listed in table 3.2. When you total 18 out of 39 possible points, advance to step 4, the volley.

Table 3.1   Scoring Summary: Beginners

Toss Drills

1. Service-toss target _____ out of 5

2. Ready, aim, throw _____ out of 5

Punch-Serve Drills

1. Service-line serves _____ out of 7

2. Target serves _____ out of 9

3. Serve and return games _____ out of 7

TOTAL _____ **out of 33**

Table 3.2   Scoring Summary: Intermediate and Advanced Players

Full-Swing Serve Drills

1. Consecutive first serves _____ out of 5

2. Serve and return games _____ out of 7

3. Advanced target serves _____ out of 9

Serve and Groundstroke Drills

1. No-ad set _____ out of 9

2. Regular set _____ out of 9

TOTAL _____ **out of 39**

Volleying to Force the Action

Now things are going to get a lot more interesting. Although you have to start building your game with the foundational forehand, backhand, and serve, learning then mastering the volley opens up a whole new approach to the game. If you have an aggressive side to your personality, the volley lets you express it. The volley offers a chance to play from anywhere on the court, to put pressure on your opponent, and to end points quickly.

Hitting a volley is as much a state of mind as it is a stroke to be mastered. You have to hit forehand and backhand groundstrokes to play the game, but in most situations you don't have to hit volleys. Hitting volleys is a choice—you have to want to get to a position in the forecourt where you can take advantage of the situation and force the action. Volleyers like to hit volleys; baseliners avoid them. For aggressive players, however, volleys are an important part of a successful offensive and defensive game plan.

You'll have to make decisions during the match about how to take advantage of situa-

tions that allow you to get to the net. Look for an opening. When your opponent hits short into your forecourt and without much pace, be ready to hit an approach shot and move into a volleying position. The approach shot is a groundstroke hit against a weak return. In most cases, hit this shot down the line, more or less parallel to the line closest to your position. Sending your approach shot down this line pins your opponent into the corner, setting you up for a winning volley. Against players who move well on the baseline, occasionally try a down-the-middle approach shot. Sending the approach shot down the middle takes away a baseliner's speed advantage and reduces his or her angle of return.

The position on the court from which volleys are hit as well as the playing level of your opponent require that the pace and location of your shots be more exact. A weak volley sets you up to lose the point on the next shot. A quick and solid stroke tells your opponent and anyone watching that they are dealing with someone who can play the entire court.

The volley is even more important in doubles, where most points are won and lost at the net. Good doubles teams get to the net together as soon as possible. Teams who don't play the net usually lose. Volleying ability often separates beginners from intermediates and intermediates from advanced players.

FOREHAND AND BACKHAND VOLLEYS

Hitting volleys correctly is not a very natural motion. The first difference with volleying is in the backswing. When you are close to the net, there is no time to take the racket back very far. The backswing on either side in volleying should be a short, restricted motion. As you see the ball coming, bring your racket back to a point not much farther than an imaginary line even with your back and parallel to the net. If an observer were to stand on the side opposite of your racket hand, he or she should not be able to see your racket as you take your backswing (figure 4.1).

Figure 4.1 Abbreviated backswing.

Backswing Drill. *Back to the Wall*

Stand with your back against a fence or a wall. A partner tosses a ball to your forehand, and you return it with a volley (figure 4.2). Don't worry about how you are holding the racket at this point. That detail will come later. Hit 10 balls this way. Avoid letting your racket touch the fence or wall when you take the racket back. Develop a habit of stepping forward with the opposite foot to hit the ball.

Figure 4.2 Back to the wall.

To Increase Difficulty

- Volley so that your partner can catch the ball without moving.
- Increase the distance between you and your partner.
- Have your partner increase the speed of the tosses.

To Decrease Difficulty

- Decrease the distance between you and your partner.
- Have your partner toss only to your forehand or only to your backhand.

Success Check

- Make the backswing short and compact.
- Step forward and away from the fence.

Score Your Success

1 to 3 successful bumps to the tosser = 1 point

4 to 7 successful bumps to the tosser = 2 points

8 to 10 successful bumps to the tosser = 3 points

Your score ____

Beginners use an eastern forehand grip for forehand shots (figure 4.3) and an eastern backhand grip for backhand shots (figure 4.4). Intermediate-level players should learn to hit with a continental grip on forehands and back- hands but allow enough flexibility to make slight adjustments, depending on the situation. For that reason, it's a good idea to grip the racket loosely enough between shots to make changes but tight enough so the racket doesn't twist on contact.

Figure 4.3 | Forehand Volley

a *b* *c*

PREPARATION

1. Eastern forehand grip for beginners; continental grip for intermediate and advanced players
2. Off hand starts on racket throat then moves out to help maintain balance
3. Knees bent; light on your feet
4. Weight forward on toes
5. Quick shoulder turn

SWING

1. Firm grip, wrist, and arm
2. Racket head at eye level
3. Step forward (not across) with opposite foot
4. Compact swing; racket face slightly open
5. Arm goes from bent position to slightly (not fully) extended position
6. Make contact to the side and in front

FOLLOW-THROUGH

1. Hit through the ball, but little or no follow-through
2. Finish with weight on front foot
3. Recover for next shot

Misstep

Contact is late.

Correction

Shorten your backswing.

Figure 4.4 Backhand Volley

a

b

c

PREPARATION

1. Eastern backhand grip for beginners; continental grip for intermediate and advanced players
2. Off hand on racket throat
3. Knees bent; light on your feet
4. Weight forward on toes
5. Quick shoulder turn

SWING

1. Firm grip, wrist, and arm
2. Racket head at eye level
3. Step forward (not across) with opposite foot
4. Blocking motion with compact swing; racket face slightly open
5. Arm goes from bent position to slightly (not fully) extended position
6. Make contact to the side and in front

FOLLOW-THROUGH

1. Hit through the ball, but with little or no follow-through
2. Finish with weight on front foot
3. Recover for next shot

Misstep

The backhand volley has no power.

Correction

Move forward as you hit. Be sure your grip is firm.

In the continental grip (figure 4.5), the wrist is directly on top of the racket handle. The thumb has to provide more support from the rear because the wrist is not positioned behind the racket. Extend your thumb along the back of the grip so the inside part of the thumb is in contact.

On many shots there isn't time to change back and forth between grips. Getting used to an all-purpose grip is difficult and not always appropriate. For example, on a high volley to the forehand side, making a slight wrist movement toward a forehand grip works, as does a move toward a backhand grip on the opposite side. The advantage of the continental grip is that it prevents having to change grips from the forehand to the backhand. The disadvantage is that some players don't have the strength the continental grip requires or they just never get comfortable with it.

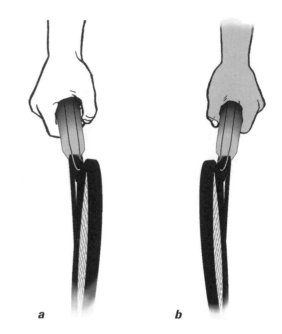

a *b*

Figure 4.5 Continental grip: *(a)* right-handed player; *(b)* left-handed player.

Grip Drill. *Hand Behind the Back*

Take a volleying position at the net with a partner at the opposite baseline. Keep the ball in play 10 times using the continental grip. Keep your other hand out of the way to avoid the temptation of changing grips and to build strength in the forearm.

To Increase Difficulty

- Put a coin between your racket handle and little finger. If the coin falls out during the preparation, you have changed grips.

To Decrease Difficulty

- Hold your free hand at your side to help maintain balance.

Success Check

- Place wrist on top of racket handle.
- Hold racket in front of body; keep racket head up.
- Keep grip tight on contact.

Score Your Success

1 to 3 successful volleys = 1 point

4 to 7 successful volleys = 3 points

8 to 10 successful volleys = 5 points

Your score ___

Approaching the net while maintaining good balance requires a move called the *split step*. The split step will help you go either left or right as your opponent gets ready to strike the ball. To practice the split step, start at the baseline. Move forward toward the net. Just before or when you reach the service line, take a short hop to square your feet to the net. Think of this hop as a hopscotch-type movement you might do on a playground. Without coming to a complete stop, move forward again to hit either a forehand or backhand volley. Timing is important. Execute your split step just a split-second before the other player strikes the ball.

Footwork Drill 1. *Attack*

Both practice partners exchange groundstrokes from their respective baselines. When either partner hits a weak shot that falls into the opposite forecourt, the player on that side hits an approach shot down the line or down the middle, takes a split step on the way to the net, and the point is on. Put the ball into play 10 times and keep score.

To Increase Difficulty

• Points are won only by hitting a winning volley (one that cannot be returned).

To Decrease Difficulty

• Have one partner start the drill by putting the ball in play with a weak setup.

Success Check

• Hit down-the-line or down-the-middle approach shots.
• Take a split step after approach shots.
• Arms and racket are up; make contact in front.

Score Your Success

1 to 3 points won = 3 points

4 to 7 points won = 5 points

8 to 10 points won = 7 points

Your score ___

Footwork Drill 2. *Toss to Volley*

Take a position 8 to 10 feet from the net, facing a partner who is close to the net on the opposite side. Have your partner soft toss 10 balls alternately to your backhand and forehand sides. Move laterally toward the net and "bump volley" the tosses back across the net. Return to the starting position after every hit.

For variety, have a partner stand about 20 feet from you and toss 10 balls to both your forehand and backhand sides. Instead of gripping the racket on the handle, choke up and hold it on the throat for more control (figure 4.6). Do not swing hard. Just bump the ball back to the tosser.

Figure 4.6 Choke up.

To Increase Difficulty

• Have your partner toss either right or left randomly.
• Have your partner increase the pace of the toss.

To Decrease Difficulty

• Have your partner toss only to your forehand side or your backhand side.
• Have your partner stand closer and toss softly.

Success Check

• Get to the ball in time to hit it at shoulder height.
• Step forward with the left foot on forehand side (righthanders); right foot forward on backhand side.

Score Your Success

1 to 3 successful bump volleys = 1 point

4 to 7 successful bump volleys = 2 points

8 to 10 successful bump volleys = 3 points

Your score ___

The swing in the volley is more of a punch, and the pace on the ball comes as much from your body's forward movement as it does from the power provided by your arm. Stand in the ready position 8 to 10 feet from the net. Move in even closer if you are hitting volleys for the first time. Keep the racket directly in front of your body, with your arms extended and your off hand on the racket throat. The racket should be in a position exactly halfway between your forehand and backhand sides. Keep your weight forward, so that your heels barely touch the court, if at all. Take a deep bend in the knees to get the feeling of hitting from a crouch. Bend forward at the waist slightly. Remember, as the ball approaches, you want to be in a position to spring forward.

If the ball comes to your right side, use your right foot to pivot. With your left foot, step forward in the direction you want to hit (figure 4.3b, the forehand volley swing, page 52). Concentrate on moving forward, not to the side. If the ball comes to your left side, pivot on the left foot, and step forward and into the ball with the right foot (figure 4.4b, the backhand volley swing, page 53). If the ball comes directly at you, slide to one side of the path of the ball by pushing off with one foot and stepping at an angle toward the net with the other. Direct shots such as these are easier to hit with a backhand than a forehand.

Watch yourself swing through forehand and backhand volleys in a mirror. Remember to look for one component of the swing at a time (e.g., footwork, grip, swinging motion). If you can't get to a mirror, visualize yourself hitting volleys. Do not keep score. Just use the activity to practice volley technique.

To be extra alert, many players crouch low and bounce on the balls of their feet when they expect a shot to be hit right at them. If the shot comes low, don't stand straight up and put the racket down to hit the ball. Instead, bend your knees even more and get down to eye level with the ball.

Throughout the entire volley motion, keep your wrist locked so that the racket forms a near 90-degree angle with your forearm. Start the stroke with your arm in a bent position, and extend the arm as you make contact. Do not extend the arm fully; you don't want to make contact with a straight, stiff arm. Lead the stroke with the racket head and dominant hand pushing forward at the same time. Swing forward from your shoulder, not your wrist or elbow. Make contact well in front of your body. Attack the ball before it attacks you.

If you have stepped forward, your weight should be on the foot closest to the net. The shoulder closest to the net should be down slightly. Direct your volleys deep into the backcourt or at an angle to pull the other player off the court.

Use a short follow-through in the direction you want to hit, but recover quickly for the next shot. Hit through the ball; do not slow your swing down before making impact. Finish the shot leaning forward with your weight on the front foot.

LOW, WIDE, AND HIGH VOLLEYS

The angle of the racket on a low volley (figure 4.7) will be open because you are bending at the knees instead of at the waist. If the low volley is slanted too far, you'll pop the ball up into the air. When you volley up, you allow your opponent to be in a position to hit a winner on the return. Even if you use perfect technique, the low volley is essentially a defensive shot. It's hard to hit winners from this position.

For low volleys, aim deep and down the line or deep and down the middle. When close to the net, practice using underspin to hit a drop volley or no spin to hit a stop volley. Get low to the ground by bending your knees. Spread

Figure 4.7 Open racket face on low volleys.

your feet to establish a low center of gravity and maintain good balance.

A high volley hit near the net is what every volleyer wants. This type of volley is the way to finish points with crisp, angled shots. If you are inside the service box and your opponent hits a return that fits the description, go for it. Rotate your shoulders early and move your feet quickly, pushing off toward the ball. Use a moderate to short backswing and a short follow-through. Go for a winner into an open corner of the court, and recovery quickly in anticipation of your opponent's next shot.

The only way to hit an effective wide volley is to move quickly as soon as you anticipate the direction of the ball or see the ball coming. If you are moving parallel to the net, it is difficult to generate any power because your weight is moving to the side, not forward. In most cases, your arm has to do more of the work to make up for the lack of forward body movement. Use a compact swing from the shoulder, and lead with the top of the racket head instead of the wrist.

Watch your opponent's racket face to anticipate the direction of his or her shot. Try to move at an angle toward the net when possible. Use your shoulder to move the racket forward as you reach. Consider returning with a crosscourt volley to the opposite side from which you are hitting. Plant your foot and recover quickly to protect the court you left open.

Volley Drill 1. *Consecutive Volleys*

Keep the ball in play by hitting 10 volleys in a row against a partner who plays groundstrokes from the baseline. This drill can be difficult but still fun. Practicing consecutive volleys helps you get used to rapid exchanges. The drill works better if your partner is an intermediate or advanced player. Practice hitting volleys deep into the backcourt.

Don't try to win points in this drill. Just get used to the idea that not only can you play at the net, you can also place the ball where you want it to go. Later, you can begin hitting volleys with pace, depth, and purpose.

Figure 4.8 Consecutive volleys.

To Increase Difficulty

- Volley against two players on the baseline, alternating volleys to each.
- Have the baseline player move inside the service line and exchange consecutive volleys (both players hitting volleys, figure 4.8).

To Decrease Difficulty

- Move back a step or two to give yourself more time to react.
- Have your partner feed only forehands or only backhands so you don't have to change grips.

Success Check

- Watch your partner's racket face at impact.
- Stay light on your feet.
- Recover quickly after each shot.

Score Your Success

1 to 3 consecutive volleys = 3 points

4 to 7 consecutive volleys = 5 points

8 to 10 consecutive volleys = 7 points

Your score ___

Volley Drill 2. *Target Volleys*

The target volleys drill is designed to help you direct volleys to specific areas of your opponent's court. Use a cardboard box or ball basket as a target, starting with the box in the deep back-court forehand corner, then in the deep backhand corner, then short and wide to the right side, and finally short and wide to the left side (figure 4.9). Your partner drops and hits 10 balls to set you up with shots to volley toward each target box.

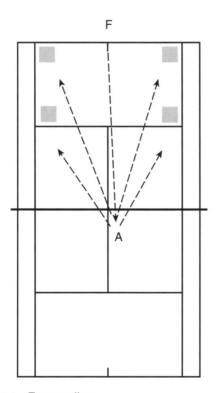

Figure 4.9 Target volleys.

To Increase Difficulty

- Hit forehand and backhand volleys alternately without changing grips.
- Move the targets to different areas.

To Decrease Difficulty

- Have your partner feed only forehand or only backhand shots.
- Use areas of the court as targets instead of boxes.

Success Check

- Hand and racket move forward together.
- Open the racket face slightly.
- Aim for an area; leave room for error.

Score Your Success

1 to 3 targets hit = 5 points

4 to 7 targets hit = 10 points

8 to 10 targets hit = 15 points

Your score ___

Volley Drill 3.   *Defend Your Turf*

Stand in one service court 8 to 10 feet from the net and defend the area between the singles sideline and the center service line (figure 4.10). Your opponent puts 10 balls into play, and you score a point every time you return a shot into your opponent's singles court.

To Increase Difficulty

- Defend the area between the doubles sideline and the center service line.

To Decrease Difficulty

- Have your partner feed balls only to your forehand side or only to your backhand side.

- Count volleys that hit within the singles or doubles boundaries.

Success Check

- Be ready to move in either direction.
- Recover quickly.

Score Your Success

1 to 3 successful volleys = 5 points

4 to 7 successful volleys = 10 points

8 to 10 successful volleys = 15 points

Your score ___

Figure 4.10   Defend your turf.

Volley Drill 4. *Volleys Win!*

As a final test, play a set against your practice partner using standard rules, with this exception: Either player who wins a point with a volley wins the game. Regardless of the score, the game is over if you or your opponent wins a point with a volley. Caution: Use good judgment when going to the net. Advance to a volleying position because your opponent is in trouble, not because you are going to take a wild chance on winning a game.

To Increase Difficulty

• Replay all points that are not won by a volley.

To Decrease Difficulty

• Play a set in which only one player has to win games by hitting winning volleys.

Success Check

• Hit groundstrokes and approach shots deep into the opposite court to open up volley opportunities.
• Use good judgment when deciding to attack.

Score Your Success

1 game won with a volley = 5 points

2 to 3 games won with volleys = 10 points

4 or more games won with volleys = 15 points

Your score ___

RETURNING VOLLEYS

In most cases, you will return your opponent's volleys with groundstrokes from the baseline area. Just as a player hitting volleys has less time to react to your shots, you will have less time to return your opponent's volleys. The first rule when returning volleys is not to panic. You don't need to hit harder or try to win the point on the first shot after your opponent has taken the net. Sometimes it takes a setup shot, then a true passing shot. Just put the ball where it will be difficult to return. You have three good return choices: a passing shot to the backhand side, a passing shot to the forehand side, or a lob over your opponent's head. If you can control the ball well enough to return it directly to your opponent, you're good enough to hit it away from the net player.

The second rule is to expect your groundstrokes to be returned quickly. Move into position and get your racket back sooner than you would during baseline exchanges. You may have to shorten your backswing if the ball is returned deep into your backcourt and with more pace than usual. Don't be surprised at quick returns; instead, learn to expect them.

Elite tennis players can predict the direction in which opponents will return the ball. This skill is called *anticipation,* and it is one of the most valuable assets a player can have. A study was conducted at the University of Illinois to determine if highly skilled players were able to use visual skills as a method of reducing reaction time to shots hit toward them. The results were reported in the *Journal of Sport & Exercise Psychology.* In the study, players volleyed balls projected at them in random directions during one trial from a ball machine and in a separate trial from an opponent. Reaction time, measured from the time the ball was projected to the time the tested players initiated racket movement, was 129 milliseconds on shots hit by an opponent and 179 milliseconds on shots projected by a machine. The investigators concluded that these players used visual skills to react to balls hit by their opponents, something they were not able to do as effectively on balls sent their way by a machine.

Although reaction time is often perceived as an inherited characteristic, this study is consistent with previous studies showing a learning element is involved in reacting to various stimuli in sports. Through experience, skilled tennis players use visual information (skill of opponent, type of shot, preparation time, position of racket face, court surface, and position of opponents' feet, to name a few) to react to and anticipate the type, direction, and velocity of balls returned to them. Although you may not yet have reached the level of a highly skilled player, it's not too early to begin developing an awareness of the factors that determine where a ball is going.

SUCCESS SUMMARY

One of the marks of a complete tennis player is the ability to use the entire court, including the area near the net. The more you practice volleys, the more comfortable you will be in the forecourt area. Try to develop a variety of volleys—offensive, defensive, high, low, wide, angled—just as you learned to hit a variety of groundstrokes.

Before beginning your work on the next step, have your practice partner or an instructor check your volley fundamentals. In the absence of an objective observer, go through your own checklist mentally. Remember these basics: short

backswing, forward movement, early contact, and tight grip. Let yourself be aggressive. When you are in a position to hit volleys, think about attacking, not defending. Try to follow the ball with your eyes all the way to the strings. Even if you think you've hit a winning volley, do not relax. Expect every shot to come back.

For each of the drills in this step, you can earn points to chart your progress. Enter your scores in table 4.1, and add them up to rate your total success. Once you have earned 27 out of the 70 points possible, go to step 5.

Table 4.1 Scoring Summary

Backswing Drill	
1. Back to the wall	_____ out of 3
Grip Drill	
1. Hand behind the back	_____ out of 5
Footwork Drills	
1. Attack	_____ out of 7
2. Toss to volley	_____ out of 3
Volley Drills	
1. Consecutive volleys	_____ out of 7
2. Target volleys	_____ out of 15
3. Defend your turf	_____ out of 15
4. Volleys win!	_____ out of 15
TOTAL	_____ *out of 70*

Hitting Half Volleys off Short Hops

The term *half volley* doesn't provide a very accurate description of this stroke—one of the most difficult to execute. The half volley is not actually a volley, but rather a forehand or backhand groundstroke hit immediately after the ball bounces onto your side of the court.

Baseball players sometimes field balls that have taken a short hop. Tennis players have to do the same thing with half volleys, but they do it with a racket instead of a glove. The only thing *half* about a half volley is the swing that is used to execute it. The half volley requircs about half the swing used for normal groundstrokes, and you have about half the normal amount of time to prepare for it.

Tennis players don't go into matches planning how they are going to use half volleys. They don't want to use them at all, in fact, unless they are forced to do so. But when those occasions arise, there are three on-the-spot tactical considerations: First, get the ball back and survive at least one more exchange. Second, get the ball back as deep into your opponent's backcourt as you can to keep your opponent from finishing you off on the next shot. And, finally, if you're really good, place the ball into an open corner

of the court to turn a bad situation into a good one.

The half volley is a necessary evil—a shot you don't want to hit very often. Once you have mastered the half volley, however, you have moved from a beginner to an intermediate or advanced level. If you have to hit a half volley, then usually one of three things has occurred:

1. You are somewhere between the baseline and service line and out of position.
2. You are late moving into position anywhere on the court.
3. Your opponent has hit a deep forcing shot that will be difficult to return.

Whatever the reason, the ball comes hard at your feet and you have to dig it out and somehow get it back. At best, the half volley is emergency tennis—like dialing 911—on the court. The goal is survival.

Young or inexperienced players often find themselves out of position because they don't know any better. Experienced players know better, but they sometimes can't do anything about it because they've lost a step or two in court coverage. Even elite players who approach the net following a serve have to hit half volleys when their opponents hit great returns at their feet. And doubles players have to play these shots all the time. Regardless of your ability level or age group, keep working on court position, but develop the skill required to hit a half volley. Read on to discover how.

HITTING A HALF VOLLEY

Because there is so little time to react, there are fewer fundamentals to master for the half volley. Start with a wide base and a quick turn of your side, or at least your shoulders, once you know the side on which you will hit the ball (figure 5.1). Don't worry about which grip to use. Just hold on tight to whatever grip you have at the moment so the racket won't twist in your hand on contact.

| Figure 5.1 | Half Volley |

a

PREPARATION
1. Early shoulder turn
2. Wide stance
3. Short backswing

b

SWING
1. Early contact
2. Firm grip
3. Block the ball

c

FOLLOW-THROUGH
1. Little or no follow-through when returning hard shots
2. Finish stroke when returning slow shots

Misstep
The grip is loose.
Correction
Hold the racket firmly on contact.

Misstep
You are overhitting the ball.
Correction
Block; don't swing.

Of all the strokes in tennis that will test your grip strength, the volley and the half volley rank at the top of the list. You can be in perfect position, you can anticipate what is about to happen, and you can be technically perfect—but if you can't hold the racket tightly enough to keep it from twisting in your hand when you are forced to hit a half volley, you'll probably mishit the shot and lose the point. Having a powerful body without a grip to match is like having a high-performance car with bald tires. Exercise equipment specialists Bert and Richard Sorin, writing for the *Strength and Conditioning Journal*, explain, "The grip is a facet of the player's strength that is usually overlooked. This becomes a weakness in the chain and an imbalance that never allows the person to perform at his or her potential."

Tennis, golf, football, wrestling, basketball, and throwing sports are among those that require substantial grip strength for the player to be effective. In some cases, the hands are the primary weapons. In others, athletes have to manipulate an object. Most sports skills that involve the hands require a combination of power and endurance.

The Sorins suggest that doing a variety of grip-strengthening activities is preferable to a single lift or exercise. They recommend gripping different oversized, soft-handle dumbbells because the hands are in a more open position as they adjust to an object. The load in these types of dumbbells is always shifting, which is similar to the shifting force of balls hitting the racket strings. "[The dumbbells are] like a stability ball for the hands," observes Richard Sorin. Adjusting other conventional exercises (shrugs, for example) to incorporate the grip is another training option. Grip-specific exercises can be used twice a week on days in which arm exercise routines are scheduled. The number of repetitions depends on the sport—low repetitions with maximal output for activities such as tennis that emphasize occasional bursts of strength and power; higher repetitions with lighter loads when grip endurance is the goal.

The most common mistakes in developing grip strength are doing too many repetitions too often and overusing one exercise. These mistakes can leave the player trained for endurance instead of power (when that is not the goal),

overtrained, or trained in a single dimension. The solution is to determine whether your sport demands power, endurance, or both, then back-engineer a program and train accordingly. The volley and half volley in tennis require a little of both: Players should train in grip-strength endurance because matches can last two or three hours, but players must also train for grip-strength power in order to handle incoming and hard-hit balls than can almost knock the racket out of your hand.

For the half volley, there isn't time to take a big backswing, so don't even try. Besides, a long backswing causes you to overhit the ball. All you need to do is block this shot (return with a short swing). As you turn your side or shoulders to the net, crouch (as though you are sitting on a stool or bench) while you hit, and stay low throughout the stroke. Get as close as you can to eye level with the ball. Block the ball to the side and in front of your position. Keep your racket head perpendicular to the court (figure 5.2). Use your off hand for support on the backhand side if it helps.

Figure 5.2 Keep the racket head perpendicular to the court on contact.

Don't worry too much about a follow-through on the half volley. Most of the time the follow-through isn't necessary when returning hard-hit shots. Aim your racket face in the direction of a target area, hold tight, and hope something good happens. On those occasions, however, when you hit half volleys on balls that don't have much pace, the follow-through is relatively normal. After a half volley, expect the worst. Hit your shot and recover immediately to the ready position for anything that comes back. If your opponent returns your shot with a weak setup, take advantage of your good fortune and go for a winner.

Half-Volley Drill 1. *Quick Hits*

One way to get used to the initial feel of a half volley is the quick-hits drill. Stand in the middle of the court a step behind the service line (figure 5.3). Drop and hit 10 shots on your forehand side, trying to make contact as quickly after the ball bounces as possible. Listen for the "bang–bang" sound of the ball first hitting the court, then striking your racket.

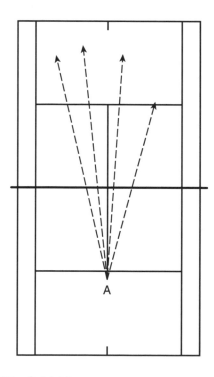

Figure 5.3 Quick hits.

To Increase Difficulty

- Direct shots alternately to the right and left sides of the opposite backcourt.

To Decrease Difficulty

- Drop and hit forehands with normal timing. Gradually decrease the time between dropping the ball and hitting it.

Success Check

- Take a wide stance
- Keep grip firm.
- Make backswing short.

Score Your Success

1 to 3 quick hits into the singles court = 1 point

4 to 7 quick hits into the singles court = 2 points

8 to 10 quick hits into the singles court = 3 points

Your score ___

Half-Volley Drill 2. *Shortstop*

Shortstop also will prepare you for hitting half volleys. Take a position right behind the baseline without your racket. Have a drill partner stand at the net and drive 10 balls toward you so they bounce several times. Move into a position in line with the ball, with your knees bent and your hands down. Field the tennis ball grounders just as a shortstop would field baseballs. Learning to handle tennis balls after they have taken short hops will prepare you for hitting half volleys.

To Increase Difficulty

- Move inside the baseline.

To Decrease Difficulty

- Have your drill partner toss balls rather than hitting them with a racket.

Success Check

- Bend more at the knees than at the waist.
- See the ball all the way into your hands.

Score Your Success

Field 1 to 3 grounders without a bobble = 1 point

Field 4 to 7 grounders without a bobble = 2 points

Field 8 to 10 grounders without a bobble = 3 points

Your score ___

Half-Volley Drill 3. *Rib Ball*

To get a feel for the restricted swinging motion of the half volley, put a ball between the inside of your hitting arm and your ribs (figure 5.4). Now practice half volleys by dropping and putting 10 balls into play. If the ball drops, your swing is too big.

To Increase Difficulty

- Keep the ball in play against a partner.

To Decrease Difficulty

- Count only the shots that hit in the opponent's backcourt.

Success Check

- Make swing tight and controlled.
- Keep racket face square to the court surface.

Score Your Success

1 to 3 shots hit into the singles court = 1 point

4 to 7 shots hit into the singles court = 2 points

8 to 10 shots hit into the singles court = 3 points

Your score ___

Figure 5.4 Rib ball.

Half-Volley Drill 4. *No-Man's-Land Rally*

Take a position between the baseline and the service line (figure 5.5). Keep the ball in play with 10 consecutive controlled shots against a partner in the same position on the opposite side of the net, with a total of 20 shots between you and your partner. Work on control even on those shots that you have to hit with half volleys. No-man's-land is not a good position for match play, but it forces you to practice shots that may help your game later. Technique is less important here than quickness.

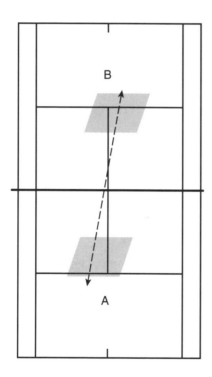

Figure 5.5 No-man's-land rally.

A good variation of the no-man's-land rally is the quick-time rally. Take a position on the baseline. Keep the ball in play 10 times each against a partner positioned very close to the net. Your partner's shots will be returned to you even faster than during the no-man's-land rally. You may have to hit some shots with volleys instead of half volleys. Anticipate where your opponent's next shot will come. Again, technique is less important than quickness.

To Increase Difficulty

• Have your partner hit from the baseline.
• Have your partner hit volleys from a position near the net.

To Decrease Difficulty

• Stand deeper in the court, near the baseline.

Success Check

• Bend more at the knees than at the waist.
• Watch the ball hit your strings.

Score Your Success

1 to 3 consecutive shots without a miss = 3 points

4 to 7 consecutive shots without a miss = 5 points

8 to 10 consecutive shots without a miss = 7 points

Your score ___

Half-Volley Drill 5. *Half-Volley Service Returns*

Have a partner practice the serve 10 times while you practice returns from one step behind the service line (figure 5.6). Serves have to be in to count. Replay faults. Change roles after each round of serves. This drill will improve your half volley, service return, and quickness.

To Increase Difficulty

- Move closer to the service line.
- Have your partner serve from a position inside the baseline.

To Decrease Difficulty

- Move two or more steps behind the service line.

Success Check

- Turn shoulders quickly.
- Make contact in front.

Score Your Success

1 to 3 successful returns = 5 points

4 to 7 successful returns = 7 points

8 to 10 successful returns = 9 points

Your score ___

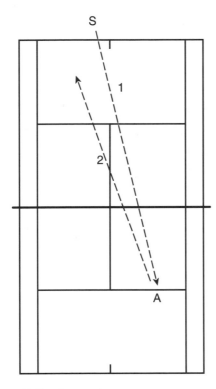

Figure 5.6 Half-volley service returns.

Half-Volley Drill 6. *Hot Seat*

Stand one step behind the service line *(A)* with a player at the baseline *(F)* behind you to feed balls (figure 5.7). Two players stand at the net opposite you. The baseline player sets up the volleyers *(B* and *C)*, who hit shots directly at you. Dig out as many shots as you can with volleys and half volleys.

To Increase Difficulty

• Stand on the service line.

To Decrease Difficulty

• Stand two to three steps behind the service line.

Success Check

• Take a crouched position.
• Hold hands and racket forward.

Score Your Success

1 to 3 successful returns = 5 points

4 to 7 successful returns = 7 points

8 to 10 successful returns = 9 points

Your score ____

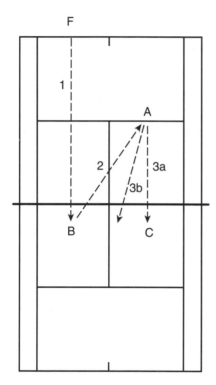

Figure 5.7 Hot seat.

SUCCESS SUMMARY

The test of your half-volley technique is whether the ball goes back over the net. The shot doesn't have to look pretty, it just has to be in. Keep your eyes wide open, turn your side early, and block the ball. Hold on tight and get the racket head low enough to dig the ball out of the court. Scraping the racket head is not a bad thing on this shot. The half volley tests your reflexes and willpower more than your skill.

Record your score for each of the drills in this step. Enter the scores in table 5.1, and add up your points to rate your total success. A total of 17 out of 34 possible points allows you to move to step 6.

Table 5.1   Scoring Summary

Half-Volley Drills	
1. Quick hits	_____ out of 3
2. Shortstop	_____ out of 3
3. Rib ball	_____ out of 3
4. No-man's-land rally	_____ out of 7
5. Half-volley service returns	_____ out of 9
6. Hot seat	_____ out of 9
TOTAL	_____ *out of 34*

Lobbing to Control Your Opponent

If you can hit forehands and backhands consistently, you are ready to hit lobs. The lob is a soft, high-arching shot, and it is one of the game's most valuable strokes. Despite the advantages of the lob, it is a shot that players seldom practice or refine. Too bad. By not working on this important skill, players are missing the chance to add another winning stroke to their arsenal. Defensive lobs extend points when you are in trouble, offensive lobs win points, and both are ways to keep your opponent off balance. Effective lobs can really distract and unnerve your opponent. Use a lob any time it can help you win a point, which is more often than most players realize.

Try a lob occasionally even if you lose the point. If nothing else, the lob will surprise your opponent. Without the threat of a lob, other players don't have to defend against the possibility. They can anticipate that you are going to keep the ball in play with normal groundstrokes; this grants them an unnecessary advantage.

Try not to overuse the lob, however. For example, don't go into a singles match thinking, *I can beat this player by lobbing.* Instead, think, *I can use the lob to win points when I'm in control of the situation, and I can use the lob to stay in the point longer when I'm in trouble.* When in control, lob to the backhand side. Don't give away your intention to lob by the way you set up. Make it look like any other shot. When scrambling to a corner, lob crosscourt. Lob low (but not too low) on offensive shots, high and deep on defensive lobs.

In doubles, include the lob in your game plan. Returning difficult serves, lobbing over the net player, and lobbing when both opponents are at the net are all part of your tactical package. Read step 10 for more about the role of the lob in doubles.

HITTING A LOB

You can hit a lob using either a forehand or a backhand. The grip for a forehand lob (figure 6.1) is the same as for a forehand groundstroke and can be an eastern, semiwestern, or western grip—your choice.

73

Figure 6.1   Forehand Lob

PREPARATION

1. Forehand grip
2. Run and plant foot
3. Short backswing on defensive lobs

SWING

1. Open racket face
2. Low-to-high swing

FOLLOW-THROUGH

1. Finish with racket high on defensive lobs
2. Complete follow-through on offensive lobs

Misstep

Lobs are short and low.

Correction

Aim for the back third of the court. Increase the length of your follow-through.

If you are hitting a defensive lob, you won't have much time to prepare. Making a short blocking motion with a firm grip and keeping your racket face open to lift the ball are about all you can do to stay in the point. If you have more time, swing with a down-to-up motion to get the ball high enough to clear an opponent at the net and deep enough to make her retreat to play the shot.

A backhand lob (figure 6.2) is hit with a backhand grip, which for most people is either a standard eastern or a modified western. Players who use a two-handed backhand may have more difficulty hitting a backhand lob because the racket is a little more difficult to maneuver on hard shots hit directly at you. When you have more time to set up for a lob, the motion again is a sweeping down-to-up path of the racket (open face) to lift the ball high and deep.

Figure 6.2 | Backhand Lob

a

PREPARATION

1. Backhand grip
2. Run and plant foot
3. Short backswing on defensive lobs

b

SWING

1. Open racket face
2. Low-to-high swing

c

FOLLOW-THROUGH

1. Finish with racket high on defensive lobs
2. Complete follow-through on offensive lobs

Misstep

Lobs are out.

Correction

Reduce the length of your backswing. Compensate for wind at your back. Don't swing as hard.

When you are defending against a smash, you don't have much choice about what to do or how to do it. Staying in the point one more shot is the goal. But when you have time to set up and your opponent is expecting a groundstroke, a well-disguised offensive lob—forehand or backhand—can win the point being played and can give your opponent something else to worry about the next time he comes to the net.

Here's how you hit a lob. First, let's discuss the easy part. Hold the racket as you would for any groundstroke, although you may have to hold it tighter just before contact with the ball to withstand the force of an opponent's smash. No special grip is required. If a shot comes to your forehand side, use the grip you have been practicing for forehand groundstrokes. Change to a one-handed or two-handed backhand to hit lobs from the opposite side. Look at it this way: The lob is just another way of executing a forehand or backhand, but it's hit higher, softer, and preferably deeper than a normal ground-stroke—if it were only that easy.

If you are at the net and your opponent tries to lob over your head, you have several options. If you can let the ball bounce without losing your offensive position, play the shot after it has bounced and return the lob with a smash. If you are very close to the net, move in and put the ball away with a smash before it bounces.

If by letting the ball bounce you would lose your attacking position, play the ball while it is in the air. If you are in a comfortable position, go for a winning shot, either short and angled to pull your opponent wide or deep to keep her in trouble. If you are not set up comfortably, return the lob into your opponent's backcourt with a controlled smash.

If you cannot hit the ball while it is in the air, turn immediately and sprint in the direction of the ball toward the baseline. Don't run directly under the ball. You have to be able to hit it with something resembling a forehand or backhand when you arrive, so move in a line parallel and to the side of the path of the ball. In other words, give yourself room to swing. Following directly under the path of the ball doesn't give you that option. If and when you catch up to the lob, return it with your own lob as high and deep as you can. At this point, you are struggling just to stay alive. Worry more about getting to the ball and lobbing than how you look doing it.

When you are in the backcourt and your opponent lobs, you can play the shot in two ways. The first is to set up and hit a controlled smash into the backcourt. The second is to return your opponent's lob with a lob of your own. *Moon-ball* rallies (lobs versus lobs) happen occasionally, but they're not very pretty and not much fun.

When was the last time you practiced your lob? "Tennis players tend to practice their strengths rather than their weaknesses," says Camille Soulier, MS, a teaching professional in Hattiesburg, Mississippi, who also coaches the men's and women's tennis teams at Pearl River Community College. Soulier describes the three basic mistakes tennis players make in training.

"Baseliners spend hours hitting ground-strokes instead of spending more of that time on serves, volleys, and overheads. Big hitters do just the opposite by practicing their power strong strokes instead of using that time to become steadier at the baseline. Neither group spends much time on specialty shots such as the lob, even though the shot comes up time after time during a match.

"The second mistake is in not practicing match situations. Left on their own, they'll usually play routine sets or matches when they could be putting themselves in circumstances that frequently occur during competition. For example, it's tough to come back when you are down 15-40 in a game, but it can be done. To prepare for playing from behind, play an entire set in practice starting each game down 15-40. It gets you accustomed to that match situation so you won't be facing it for the first time in a real match. It will also surprise you how many times you can come back and win those games.

"The third mistake I see in practice is a reluctance to play sets and matches at a lesser level. It is natural to want every match to be a thing of beauty to play and to watch, but it's not realistic. Lots of matches, especially those against slightly less skilled opponents, are ugly. The better player gets dragged down to a level that is not comfortable and has trouble just grinding it out and taking a win, ugly or not. You can't go to practice and deliberately play poorly, but you can make winning points harder. Try playing an entire set in which a point cannot be won until the ball has been in play six times. In other words, the point starts on the seventh shot. That will force you to be patient instead of trying textbook-perfect shots to win the point right away."

Lob Drill. *Drop-and-Hit Lobs*

Start practicing the lob with a simple drop-and-hit lobs drill. Stand just behind the baseline (figure 6.3). Drop a ball to your forehand side and hit a normal groundstroke to your partner, who is positioned 8 to 10 feet from the net. Continue hitting, but each time increase the height and arc of the ball until you are comfortably clearing your partner, who is now extending the racket high above his or her head. The drill starts when you are ready to hit 10 consecutive lobs. Count the number of times your shot clears the racket and lands in the backcourt area. If you don't have a practice partner, stand in the parking lot behind a court with a basket of balls. Drop and hit lobs over the fence into the playing area.

To Increase Difficulty

- Allow your partner to smash any lob hit too low.
- Try the same drill with backhand lobs.

To Decrease Difficulty

- Execute the drill without a practice partner.

Success Check

- Take swing path low to high.
- Open the racket face.

Score Your Success

1 to 3 successful lobs = 1 point

4 to 7 successful lobs = 2 points

8 to 10 successful lobs = 3 points

Your score ___

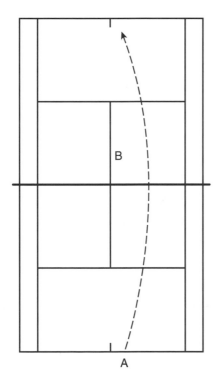

Figure 6.3 Drop-and-hit lobs.

DEFENSIVE LOB

The hard part about hitting a lob is preparing to hit a defensive lob. The truth is, if you are scrambling to survive a point, preparation is seldom the same, and fundamentals take second place to returning the ball high and deep any way you can. Points are not awarded for style. If you have time to set up perfectly with your feet, grip, and backswing, you probably shouldn't be hitting a lob in the first place.

Nevertheless, consider these techniques when hitting a defensive lob. The first is footwork. Quickly step out and back with the foot on the same side as your dominant arm. Focus on the ball, but turn your shoulders in the direction you're moving. Anytime you are in trouble on the court, shorten your backswing. If the other player has hit the ball hard enough, you may be able to just block the ball upward to return it. One other suggestion to escape from trouble: Direct your lobs crosscourt to reduce the amount of open court to which your opponent can smash. Open the racket face slightly. Lift the ball with a low-to-high swing. Get it well into the air so you'll have enough time to recover and get back into position for the next shot. If you can, follow through to ensure depth on your return. The follow-through will be up and out, away from your body. A full follow-through will help you get the feel of gently lifting the ball into the air and deep into the backcourt. If you make a mistake, make it too deep or too high rather than too short and too low.

Defensive Lob Drill 1. *Lob–Smash Warm-Up*

With a skilled partner or instructor, try the lob–smash warm-up. Stand behind the baseline, and put the ball into play 10 times with a lob. Your partner at the net hits controlled smashes directed toward your position. Continue the rally, using only controlled lobs and return smashes. Count the number of successful lob–smash combinations. Intermediate and advanced players often use this exercise as part of a warm-up.

To Increase Difficulty

• Count only the number of times two consecutive lob–smash combinations are completed.

To Decrease Difficulty

• Start over after each two-shot lob–smash combination.

Success Check

• Use a delicate touch.
• Block or deflect.

Score Your Success

1 to 3 successful lob–smash combinations = 3 points

4 to 7 successful lob–smash combinations = 5 points

8 to 10 successful lob–smash combinations = 7 points

Your score ___

Defensive Lob Drill 2.   *Chase It Down*

Have a partner stand at the net and alternately drive 10 shots to your forehand and backhand corners (figure 6.4). Move to the ball, and return shots with lobs. Take short steps to get started, and then shift to high gear to run toward the ball. Don't concentrate as much on technique as on chasing down the ball and staying in the point for one more shot. Aim most lobs crosscourt.

To Increase Difficulty

- Play the point out after the lob; don't take a break before the next sequence.

To Decrease Difficulty

- Have your partner feed shots only to your forehand corner; later, only to your backhand side.

Success Check

- Take a quick start.
- Move racket back early.
- Aim high and deep.

Score Your Success

1 to 3 successful lobs = 3 points

4 to 7 successful lobs = 5 points

8 to 10 successful lobs = 7 points

Your score ___

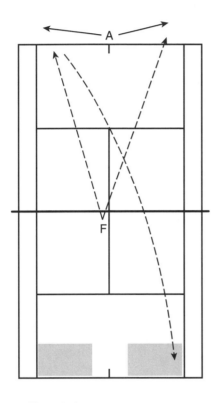

Figure 6.4   Chase it down.

OFFENSIVE LOB

The offensive lob is designed to win the point by using a shot your opponent doesn't expect. When your opponent expects you to hit a passing shot, an offensive lob will catch the other player off guard, sending the ball over his or her head for a winner.

Prepare to hit the offensive lob by making it look like any other groundstroke. If you give the preparation a different look, the opponent will anticipate what you are going to do and get into a position to smash your lob. The downside of the offensive lob is that the opportunity to use it presents itself infrequently, and the shot requires more timing and touch than most players are able to master. The offensive lob is not for beginners, but intermediate players can begin to experiment with it.

Advanced players occasionally hit a topspin lob by rapidly brushing the back of the ball with an almost upward motion, racket face perpendicular to the court. An effective topspin lob clears the opponent's outstretched racket, bounces, and picks up speed as the ball moves away from the hitter and toward the back of the court.

For offensive lobs that don't have exaggerated topspin, open the racket face to direct the ball up. The point of contact may be farther back in relationship to your body than on other shots because you are returning a forcing shot and because waiting another fraction of a second usually means your opponent will be committed even closer to the net. With an open racket face and a low-to-high swing, lift the ball upward and hit it up to clear your opponent's outstretched racket. The ball should be high enough so she can't reach it before the bounce and deep enough so it cannot be returned after the bounce (figure 6.5). If you have a choice, hit to the backhand side.

Follow through in the direction you are attempting to hit. The follow-through on the lob may not be as complete as on other shots, but don't restrict this part of the stroke deliberately. Instead, hold the racket firmly, keep your wrist steady, and try to carry the ball on your strings as long as possible. If you think too much about

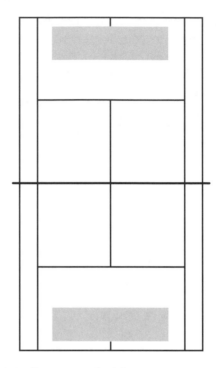

Figure 6.5 Target areas for lobs.

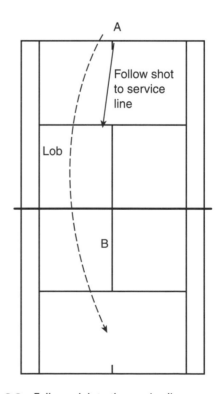

Figure 6.6 Follow a lob to the service line.

shortening the follow-through, you may begin to slow down your racket speed before contact.

After a successful offensive lob, follow the line of your shot and move forward to the service line (figure 6.6). If your opponent does get to the ball, he will return it with a lob. If you stay on the baseline, you lose your offensive position. If you go all the way to the net, however, a good lob will put you on the defensive again. From the service line you will have time to move closer to the net for a point-ending smash. If your lob is returned deep into your backcourt, you will still be in position to move back and hit a smash in the air or after the ball has bounced on your side.

Offensive Lob Drill 1. *Moon-Ball Rally*

To practice offensive lobs, take a position on the baseline opposite a practice partner for a moon-ball rally (figure 6.7). Keep the ball in play 10 times each with lobs, also known as *moon balls*. Count the number of successful lobs hit into the backcourt. The first shot is a setup lob. Scoring starts on the second shot.

To Increase Difficulty

- Count only shots that land within 10 feet of the baseline.

To Decrease Difficulty

- Perform the drill in three-shot sequences (setup, lob return, another lob return), and then start again.

Success Check

- Think deep.
- Aim to the backhand side.

Score Your Success

1 to 3 successful moon balls = 3 points

4 to 7 successful moon balls = 5 points

8 to 10 successful moon balls = 7 points

Your score ___

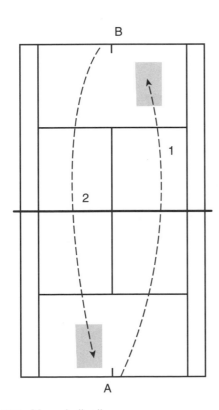

Figure 6.7 Moon-ball rally.

Offensive Lob Drill 2. *Lob Retreat*

For the lob retreat drill, take a position at the net. Your partner stands at the baseline and lobs 10 balls over your head. Turn and run to the side of the flight of the ball, and return it (make a *get*) with a forehand or backhand lob once you catch up to it. Your partner follows the line of the lob, moves in near the service line, and attempts to finish the point with a volley or smash.

To Increase Difficulty

- Play the point out before continuing the sequence.

To Decrease Difficulty

- Have your partner hit higher to allow you time to reach the ball.

Success Check

- Run to the side of the path of the ball.
- Lob high and deep.

Score Your Success

1 to 3 successful gets = 3 points

4 to 7 successful gets = 5 points

8 to 10 successful gets = 7 points

Your score ___

Offensive Lob Drill 3. *Lob–Smash Game*

Stand at the baseline and put a lob into play against an opponent who begins the game in a forecourt volleying position. Only lobs and smashes are allowed. The first player to make 10 points wins the game; then switch roles. Remember to follow successful lobs (over your opponent's head) to the service line. Then be ready to move in even closer for a smash or retreat to retrieve a lob deep into your backcourt.

To Increase Difficulty

- Try to protect the doubles court instead of the singles area.
- Award 2 points to the player hitting smashes, 1 point to the player hitting lobs.

To Decrease Difficulty

- Protect only half the court, from the center mark to the singles sideline.

- Award 2 points to the player hitting lobs, 1 point to the player hitting smashes.

Success Check

- Block the smash with a firm grip and open racket face.
- Lob high enough to clear the net player and deep enough to make him or her retreat.

Score Your Success

1 to 3 games won = 5 points

4 to 7 games won = 7 points

8 to 10 games won = 9 points

Your score ___

SUCCESS SUMMARY

Use the groundstroke grips you have been practicing, and shorten your backswing. If you are in trouble, fight to stay alive even if your technique suffers. Winning a match is war, not a beauty contest. Remember: Practice quick feet, an open racket face, a low-to-high swing, and enough follow-through to get the ball deep.

Look back at your scores for the six lob drills. Enter your scores for each drill in table 6.1, and add them up to rate your total success. If you score 21 out of a possible 40 points, advance to the next step.

Table 6.1 Scoring Summary

Lob Drill	
1. Drop-and-hit lobs	_____ out of 3
Defensive Lob Drills	
1. Lob–smash warm-up	_____ out of 7
2. Chase it down	_____ out of 7
Offensive Lob Drills	
1. Moon-ball rally	_____ out of 7
2. Lob retreat	_____ out of 7
3. Lob–smash game	_____ out of 9
TOTAL	_____ *out of 40*

Smashing the Overhead Shot With Authority

You've done everything right so far. Strong groundstrokes put your opponent in a defensive position. Your approach shot pinned her to the corner. A strong volley should have won the point, but she managed to chase it down. Now she puts up a weak lob and you're ready to finish the point.

This is the perfect scenario for an overhead smash—an aggressive, offensive, hard shot usually hit from the forecourt. The opportunity to smash doesn't always happen this way, but when it does, here's how to execute the shot. What you do with overhead smashes depends on court position. Inside the service boxes, go for winners by hitting into the open part of the court and away from your opponent. When your opponent begins to anticipate where you are going to hit, hit behind him. On those occasions when the lob goes deep and you have enough time to get back and let the ball bounce, go for the angled winner or hit deep into the open corner. There also will be times when you are forced to hit smashes even though you are in a defensive position. Here the idea is to get the ball back, send it as deep as possible, and hit your mental "rewind" to position yourself for the rest of the point.

HITTING AN OVERHEAD SMASH

The showtime part of an overhead smash comes when the racket face crushes the ball for a winner. The working end of a smash begins with the feet. Remember these three words when you go for the overhead smash: Move your feet! The player who digs in to a position too early while waiting for a lob to come down is in trouble. Many things can alter the expected flight path of the ball—wind, spin, misjudged trajectory or velocity—and create problems for the player who assumes a fixed position. Take lots of little steps to get into position, get the racket back and behind your head, and try to shift your weight forward with your swing. When you make contact, your arm should be extended as high as you can reach and slightly in front of your body.

The grip on the overhead smash must be either an eastern forehand or a continental. Any other grip will prohibit you from striking the ball as hard as you should. And, by rotating your wrist just before contact, you can hit this shot either flat (with no spin) and forcefully or with spin to make the ball move away from your opponent.

Be aggressive with the smash, but don't assume it's a going to be a winner. It's okay to hit a first smash as a setup for the kill on the second one. Either way, the objective is to finish the point.

Beginners and intermediates may hold the racket with a forehand grip for the overhead smash, but almost all advanced players use a continental grip (figure 7.1). As with a serve, the continental grip allows you to snap your wrist on impact with the ball, and it gives you some choices about what to do with the ball, like hitting it flat (no spin), hitting it with spin, or hitting it inside out instead of across your body.

Figure 7.1   Overhead Smash

PREPARATION

1. Short, quick steps; feet staggered like a quarterback setting up to pass
2. Hips and shoulders sideways to the net
3. Abbreviated backswing; racket back early (on lobs that bounce, you may have time for a full backswing)
4. Continental grip
5. Ball in front of body; opposite hand pointing to ball

SWING

1. Reach high to hit; contact up and in front of body
2. Rotate hips and shoulders
3. Snap wrist at contact
4. Close to the net, go for the winner
5. Away from the net, go for placement

FOLLOW-THROUGH

1. Swing through the shot
2. Racket moves away from body, across, then down
3. Move closer to net in case opponent returns your smash

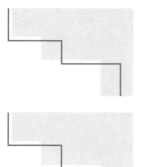

Misstep

The smash lacks power.

Correction

Make contact in front of your body.

Misstep

Smashes go into the net.

Correction

Don't let the ball drop too low. Reach up to hit with your arm extended.

Because the continental grip is as close to the backhand as it is to the forehand, and because you hit the smash on the forehand side of your body, you have to make some adjustments. The main adjustment is rotating your wrist outward just before contact (figure 7.2). During an outward rotation or wrist snap, when looking at the back of your hand, your thumb will go away from your body across and down. The pronation in the wrist allows you to hit the ball flat and with more pace than you would on groundstrokes. If you don't snap your wrist, the shot will have too much spin and not enough velocity, although there are times when smashes should be hit with spin to make the ball curve away and out of the reach of an opponent.

To practice the wrist snap, stand close enough to the net to touch it with an overhead smash motion. Start with your racket cocked behind your head. Now swing upward, but just before the imaginary contact point rotate your wrist outward and snap down so that both side edges of your racket frame hit the top of the net at the same time. In other words, slap the net with your racket face. If you do it correctly, you should hear a cracking, smacking sound on contact.

Poor footwork is a common mistake when hitting the smash, even at the elite level. Too many players see a lob coming, dig into a fixed position, and then try to hit. Because lobs suspend in the air longer than other shots, however, variables such as velocity, spin, and trajectory may change during the flight of the ball. If you set too soon, you might misread some of those variables and fail to make the needed adjustments. Take several short half- and quarter- steps while preparing to hit. Keeping your feet active will help you be in the perfect active position to hit when the time comes.

As soon as you see that you can hit a smash, turn your side to the net so that one foot is forward and one is back, as in the serve. A right-handed player puts the right foot back and the left foot forward. For a left-handed player, the left foot goes back and the right foot goes forward. As you hit, push off with the back foot and transfer your weight forward.

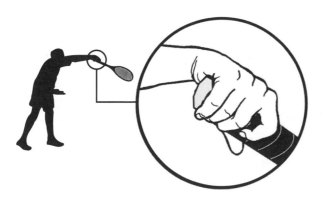

Figure 7.2 Wrist snap.

Footwork Drill. *Shadow Smash and Touch*

Start at the net, turn, move back quickly (take two to three steps), plant the back foot, and swing through the smash motion without hitting the ball. Then move forward immediately to touch the net with your racket. Complete the series of up-and-back movements 10 times.

To Increase Difficulty

- Retreat to the service line after each net touch.

To Decrease Difficulty

- Execute the drill in slow motion until you feel more comfortable with the routine.

Success Check

- Be quick in the feet.
- Keep the side always toward the net when moving back.

Score Your Success

1 to 3 successful sequences = 1 point

4 to 7 successful sequences = 2 points

8 to 10 successful sequences = 3 points

Your score ___

To prepare for the smash, bring the racket up directly in front of your body, then take it to a position behind your head. Tip the racket up. By eliminating the full swing, you can reduce the margin of error. If you have a good court position, you can generate enough power to put the ball away or hit to an open area.

On the rare occasions when the ball bounces and you have plenty of time for a full swing, drop the racket down as you would on a serve, bring it up behind your back, and let it fly. You can get even more power with a full backswing, but the shot will be less efficient and less accurate than with a restricted backswing.

Most tennis instructors tell their students to point to the ball with the off hand as they get the racket back. This motion may not feel natural, and it will take time to develop the technique. Pointing can improve concentration and make you aware of your position in relation to the ball. Use the pointing technique only if it helps you

hit better smashes. Pointing is not an essential fundamental for this stroke.

The overhead smash swing motion is similar to a forceful punch serve. Bring your racket up and forward as if throwing it across the net. Reach as high as you can to make contact. As you swing, shift your weight forward. Hit the ball at a point in front of your body. As you hit, rotate your wrist outward and snap down with the thumb. If you are close to the net, hit the ball with as little spin as possible to get maximum velocity. If you are at midcourt, use spin to make the ball curve down and into the court. If you are in the backcourt, also use spin. The distance between you and your opponent in this last situation is too far for a flat shot to be effective. Follow through out, down, and across your body. Bring the racket through the stroke naturally, and return it to the ready position for the next shot. Never assume that your shot will be the last one in an exchange.

Smash Drill 1. *Self-Toss*

Stand near the net, holding your racket in a cocked position. Toss 10 consecutive balls forward slightly and high into the air. With each toss, reach high and hit a smash. Keep the ball in front of your position on the court, and don't allow the ball to drop too low. Try to make the ball bounce high into the opposite court so that an opponent would not be able to make a return.

To Increase Difficulty

- Toss the ball higher or farther behind your head.
- Practice against an opponent who tries to return your smashes.

To Decrease Difficulty

- Practice technique, not power.

Success Check

- Extend arm upward.
- Snap wrist on contact.

Smash Drill 2.   *Lob–Smash Combination*

Now you are ready for some live-fire drills. Have a partner or instructor hit short setup lobs from the baseline (figure 7.3). Start the drill from a volleying position, and return 10 lobs directly at the feeder. Reverse roles after each series of lobs and smashes.

To Increase Difficulty

- Direct your smashes away from the feeder but into the singles court.
- Play the point out after each smash.

To Decrease Difficulty

- Stand closer to the net and have your partner hit the lobs lower.

Success Check

- Keep opposite shoulder toward the net until you are ready to swing.
- Hold head up while hitting.

Score Your Success

1 to 3 successful smashes = 3 points

4 to 7 successful smashes = 5 points

8 to 10 successful smashes = 7 points

Your score ___

Figure 7.3   Lob–smash combination.

Smash Drill 3. *Smash to Targets*

This drill will test your ability to direct smashes to specific areas of the court. Have your practice partner feed 10 lobs from the baseline. Return the lobs with smashes directed at large boxes or other targets placed in these positions: deep left corner, deep right corner, right side service box corner, and left side service box corner (figure 7.4). You can choose your target, but count the smash as successful only when a target is hit.

To Increase Difficulty

- Use smaller targets.
- Direct shots to a different target with each smash.

To Decrease Difficulty

- Direct shots to the same target with each smash.
- Use larger targets.
- Direct shots to an area of the court.

Success Check

- Align your feet in the direction of the target.
- Concentrate on control, not power.

Score Your Success

1 to 3 successful smashes = 5 points

4 to 7 successful smashes = 7 points

8 to 10 successful smashes = 9 points

Your score ___

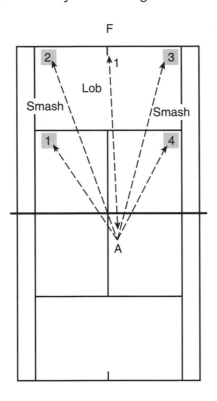

Figure 7.4 Smash to targets.

Smash Drill 4. *Smash–Volley Combination*

Smashes are often followed by put-away volleys. To practice the smash–volley combination, have a partner stand at the baseline with a basket of balls. Start near the net, and move into position to smash 10 lobs fed by your partner. After each smash, move forward for a winning volley against a short drive set up by your partner with a second ball.

To Increase Difficulty

- Have your partner hit deeper lobs or wider setups on the second feed.
- Count combinations as successful only when your volleys are clear winners.

To Decrease Difficulty

- Don't keep score; just hit the two required shots.

Success Check

- Recover quickly.
- Hold arms and racket up and in front for the volley.

Score Your Success

1 to 3 successful smash–volley combinations = 5 points

4 to 7 successful smash–volley combinations = 7 points

8 to 10 successful smash–volley combinations = 9 points

Your score ___

Smash Drill 5. *Lobbing and Smashing*

It's time to put everything together for lob–smash games. Take a position at the net, and have your partner stand at or slightly behind the baseline. Start each point with a lob. Smash the lob, and play the point out. Only the first two shots have to be a lob and a smash, respectively. After the first lob and smash, anything goes. The first player to win 10 points wins the game.

To Increase Difficulty

- Allow your partner to start the point with a deeper lob.
- Earn a point only when your smash finishes the exchange.

To Decrease Difficulty

- Have your partner start the point with a shallow, low lob.

- Score 2 points instead of 1 for every winning smash.

Success Check

- Smash wide to open up the court for the next shot.
- Don't smash to the same spot on consecutive shots.

Score Your Success

1 to 3 games won = 5 points

4 to 7 games won = 7 points

8 to 10 games won = 9 points

Your score ___

RETURNING THE OVERHEAD SMASH

When you return an overhead smash, anything goes. Reaction time, anticipation, and luck are more important than technique when returning a smash. Forget success checks. Concentrate on survival techniques! Get the ball back any way you can. In most cases, this means trying to return the smash with a high, deep defensive lob. Bargain for time and one more chance to stay in the point.

Try to anticipate where the smash will be hit so you can get a head start on chasing down the ball. Many players develop a pattern of hitting smashes to the same area of the court. When you observe a pattern of smashes, you can make an educated guess as to the direction of your opponent's next shot. Don't stand still and hope the ball comes close. As the other player smashes the ball, make a commitment and go to where you think the ball is headed, even if you occasionally move in the wrong direction.

Hold your racket even tighter than you hold it on volleys. You will have no time for a backswing. Find a way to get to the ball and block it back with the open face of your racket. If you are good enough or lucky enough to return a smash, recover immediately. Another one is probably on the way.

If your opponent makes a mistake and hits a smash that can be returned with a groundstroke, don't overreact. Inexperienced players have a tendency to try to blast the ball with a forehand or backhand once they realize they're still in the point and the ball is not coming as fast as anticipated. Take that extra split-second, measure the ball, and go for a passing shot.

SUCCESS SUMMARY

Most players enjoy hitting a smash. You can hit the ball hard and finish a point, one way or the other. The key is preparation. Take lots of quick, short steps to move into the best position. Move the racket back early, and keep the ball in front of your body. No matter how hard your smash, it may not be a winner. As soon as you hit to the open court, follow the line of your shot toward the net and recover for the possibility of another lob or an attempted passing shot.

This step describes six drills for perfecting the smash. Enter your scores for each drill in table 7.1, and add them up to rate your total success. Score at least 20 points before going to step 8.

Table 7.1   Scoring Summary

Footwork Drill	
1. Shadow smash and touch	_____ out of 3
Smash Drills	
1. Self-toss	_____ out of 3
2. Lob–smash combination	_____ out of 7
3. Smash to targets	_____ out of 9
4. Smash–volley combination	_____ out of 9
5. Lobbing and smashing	_____ out of 9
TOTAL	_____ *out of 40*

Executing Drop Shots Effectively

Which shot can you use to catch your opponent off guard? Is it another groundstroke? Should you try an approach shot? What about a drive deep into the backcourt? No. The answer is a well-planned, beautifully disguised, and perfectly executed drop shot that wins the point.

Hit a drop shot when you are positioned in the forecourt. The ball will float softly into your opponent's forecourt and bounce twice before he can get to it. The drop shot is typically hit after a series of strokes and when the opponent expects a hard, deep, driving shot. Although any player can use it, a well-hit drop shot is a relatively sophisticated stroke used by intermediate and advanced players.

The drop shot is especially effective against players who are out of position, out of shape, slow, and uncomfortable at the net. It also works against opponents who are tired, lazy, or both. That's a lot of market potential. If you use the drop shot often enough, your opponent's concern that you might use it again can make other shots from a similar position on the court become more effective. The drop shot also causes opposing players to lose their sense of rhythm.

The drop shot is all about shot selection, court position, and deception. Shot selection means hitting the ball at the right time—that is, when your opponent is out of position and not expecting it. Court position is simple. Don't try a drop shot from your baseline; from this position the drop shot has little chance of success. Deception is the fun part. Hitting a drop shot when your opponent expects you to drive the ball deep means you are winning the mental game of tennis as well as the physical game.

Be sure to use drop shots occasionally even if doing so sometimes means losing a point. The drop shot shows that you have a full bag of tricks and that you are not afraid to use all of them. Just like other strokes and their variations, the drop shot gives you one more option, and your opponents, one more problem. In tennis, you will be rewarded for being deceptive.

INCORPORATING A NEW SKILL

The drop shot definitely falls into the category of a new skill. Unlike frequently used strokes such as the forehand, backhand, and serve, learning how and when to use the drop shot generally happens later in a tennis player's development.

Incorporating any new skill, including the drop shot, into a sport you already play requires a progression of learning activities. Sport psychologist Jim Loehr, EdD, says that professional athletes need about two months of daily practice to make a change. Recreational athletes may need more time.

The first step in learning a new skill is to get a coach, teaching professional, or friend who has mastered the skill to work with you on breaking it down into its components. Someone who can see only the big picture (for example, only observing that a serve goes in or out) is of little help. A skilled observer or teacher can watch for the correct positioning of hands, feet, head, or any other part of the body instead of focusing on the end result.

The second step, visualizing and then shadow practicing the skill, is skipped by many players but can be a valuable tool in the learning process. This step has two parts. The first part is to imagine yourself executing the drop shot. See yourself take the shot in your mind, imagining how you would execute each element of the stroke. You can practice self-visualization on a tennis court, in your car, at home, or any time you have a few moments to see yourself executing the skill. A great deal of research supports using visualization as a mechanism for improved performance. If visualization is not one of your skills, get someone to videotape a technique you have been practicing, and then view it to create a mental map of the elements of the technique.

The second part of this step involves actually going through the motions by yourself, much like a boxer going through a shadow-boxing sequence in a ring. Practicing in this manner takes a dedicated athlete, one who is secure enough to tolerate the curious looks that will come when others see you playing an imaginary game. If space permits, try going through the new motion in front of a mirror at home or in a locker room. This scenario is more private and allows you to be your own coach.

The third step involves working on the new skill by simulating game situations during practice. The soccer player develops a move to get open for a pass. The swimmer makes a perfect turn off the wall. The golfer hits out of a trap and gets close enough to the hole to save a par. Likewise, the tennis player maneuvers an opponent into a position in which a drop shot wins the point. The idea is not to play out the whole game but instead to repeatedly rehearse the situation in which a newly acquired skill can be used.

The fourth step is to try out the new skill in real but unimportant games, matches, or situations. At every level, opportunities exist for experimentation when little or nothing is at stake. You have to be comfortable with the idea that you may hit a terrible drop shot or lose to an inferior opponent because you are taking time to develop a new part of your game.

Finally, the last step is to be confident enough to make the new skill an automatic response in pressure situations. If you have to think about doing the drop shot first, it's not ready for prime time. At this point, you no longer analyze, plan, or experiment. Like any other tool in your kit, the new skill is simply there at your disposal when you need it.

HITTING THE DROP SHOT

Make the drop shot (figure 8.1) look like any other stroke hit from the forecourt. To disguise the shot, don't exaggerate the backswing, delay the stroke, or change footwork. Hold the racket firmly, but not overly tight, and open the racket face. Some players change to a continental grip just before they hit to comfortably give the racket face a chance to open up.

Figure 8.1   Drop Shot

PREPARATION	SWING	FOLLOW-THROUGH
1. Forehand or backhand grip 2. Disguise the shot	1. Open racket face 2. High-to-low swing 3. Slower racket head speed 4. Backspin on the ball	1. Abbreviated swing after contact 2. Anticipate the next shot

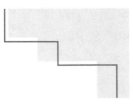

Misstep

The shot is hit too hard or too deep.

Correction

Open the racket face more.

Misstep

Points are lost attempting drop shots.

Correction

Be selective about when to use the shot.

Start with the racket head above waist level, and swing down behind the ball. Delicately slide the racket under the ball as you make contact. Slow down the speed of your swing. Take a high-to-low swing and open up the racket face to give the shot a bit of backspin. Putting backspin on the ball should make it bite into the court and slow down.

Hit the drop shot at the top of the bounce so that the ball falls downward as it clears the net. Barely clearing the net is effective but not absolutely necessary. Avoid hitting the ball so that it travels too far toward your opponent after the bounce. Ideally, the ball should move away from him or her after the bounce.

Abbreviate your follow-through. The path of the racket will slide down more than forward. Drop volleys (drop shots hit with volleys) are also more effective if the follow-through is not pronounced. Whatever you do, avoid drop shots from a position behind your baseline. Such shots will give your opponent too much time to recognize the shot and get to the ball.

Expect the other player to get to the ball and to return it. If it isn't returned, you win the point. If it is, you should be near the net and ready to volley the ball for a winner. Hitting drop shots on consecutive points may be a good idea if the other player has to work hard to reach the ball on the first drop shot.

Drop-Shot Drill 1. *Drop-and-Hit Drop Shots*

Stand where the service line intersects the center service line. Drop 10 consecutive balls and hit them with a forehand into either service court across the net. Make each shot look as much like your normal forehand preparation and swing as possible. Consider the drop shot successful if the ball bounces twice in the opposite court before passing the service line.

To Increase Difficulty

- Alternately hit shots to the opposite left and right service courts.
- Attempt half your shots with a backhand.

To Decrease Difficulty

- Have a partner softly toss balls to your forehand side.

Success Check

- Open the racket face.
- Disguise the preparation.

Score Your Success

1 to 3 successful drop shots = 3 points
4 to 7 successful drop shots = 5 points
8 to 10 successful drop shots = 7 points
Your score ___

Drop-Shot Drill 2. *Drop-Shot Setups*

Stand in the center of the court just behind the service line. Have your partner drop and hit 10 shots from his or her baseline that bounce softly between you and the net. Return each setup with a forehand drop shot that bounces twice before crossing the opposite service line (figure 8.2).

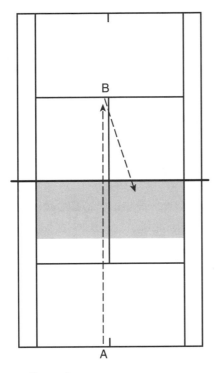

Figure 8.2 Drop-shot setups.

To Increase Difficulty

• Have your partner hit setups randomly to your forehand and backhand sides.

To Decrease Difficulty

• Have your partner move forward to the service line area and hit softer setups.

• Have your partner toss setups instead of hitting them.

Success Check

• Keep the racket-head speed slow.
• Make the backspin noticeable.

Score Your Success

1 to 3 successful drop shots = 3 points

4 to 7 successful drop shots = 5 points

8 to 10 successful drop shots = 7 points

Your score ___

Drop-Shot Drill 3. *Drop-Shot Points*

Stand behind the service line, and have a partner stand at the opposite baseline. Your partner drops and hits 10 shots into the forecourt. Return with a drop shot and play out the point.

To Increase Difficulty

• Allow your opponent to start the drill one step in front of the baseline.

To Decrease Difficulty

• Change the rules to allow the player at the net to hit any shot, including a drop shot, to prevent the baseline player from anticipating the next shot.

Success Check

• Don't tip the shot.
• Vary the location.

Score Your Success

1 to 3 points won = 3 points

4 to 7 points won = 5 points

8 to 10 points won = 7 points

Your score ___

Drop-Shot Drill 4. *Short Game*

Play a 10-point game against your partner using only drop shots (figure 8.3). Any ball hit hard or

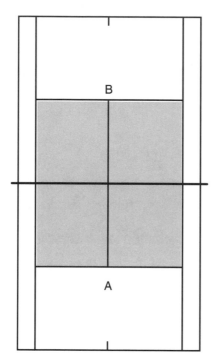

Figure 8.3 Short game.

that bounces outside the service court is out of play. Put the ball into play with a soft drop-and-hit forehand.

To Increase Difficulty

- One player hits all down-the-line drop shots; the other hits all crosscourt drop shots.

To Decrease Difficulty

- Instead of competing for points, work with your partner to see how many consecutive drop shots you can both hit.

Success Check

- Recover quickly.
- Use your off hand to adjust grips.

Score Your Success

1 to 3 games won = 3 points

4 to 7 games won = 5 points

8 to 10 games won = 7 points

Your score ___

Drop-Shot Drill 5. *Drop Shots Win!*

Play a set against a partner. If either player hits a winning drop shot from the forecourt area, the game is over. Regardless of the previous score, the player hitting the drop shot wins the game. Don't try the shot just to win a point or the game. Try the drop shot when you are positioned near the net and your partner is too far away to get to it.

To Increase Difficulty

- Players must attempt at least one drop shot per game. If not, repeat the game.
- Award a game only when a drop shot bounces twice before the opponent reaches the ball.

To Decrease Difficulty

- Allow the player hitting the drop shot to use the alleys as well as the service courts as target areas.

Success Check

- Take a quick first step.
- Hold your shot until your opponent commits.

Score Your Success

1 to 2 games won with drop shots = 5 points

3 to 4 games won with drop shots = 7 points

5 to 6 games won with drop shots = 9 points

Your score ___

RETURNING THE DROP SHOT

Players often tip off drop shots by changing their stroke or their body language. By observing how your opponent prepares and hits this shot compared to the way he or she normally hits groundstrokes, you might be able to outguess your opponent and get to the ball for a winner.

If your opponent is in the forecourt and in a position to hit a variety of shots, you must at least be aware that the drop shot is a possibility. This is especially true if you are well behind the baseline or wide to either side. Make the other player prove that he or she can hit this shot before trying to anticipate it. One successful drop shot is acceptable. If you keep getting beaten by the shot, then it's your fault.

As soon as you realize the drop shot is coming, start moving toward the ball as fast as you can. If you get there quickly, put it down the line for a winner. If you have to stretch at the last second, consider returning it over your opponent's head with a lob. Returning a drop

shot with a lob is difficult, but the lob may be your best shot because the face of your racket is already open and your forward movement can carry the ball deep. If you attempt the lob and it goes short, duck.

The third option is a tricky one—returning the drop shot with a drop shot. There are two situations in which a drop shot return might, and *might* is the operative word, be effective. The first is if your opponent hits a drop shot, anticipates a lob, and starts moving back to cover. If your touch is delicate enough to execute the shot, the other player will not be able to recover quickly enough to change directions back toward the net. As for the second situation, you can experiment with hitting a sharply angled drop shot away from an opponent who is close to the net but moving the wrong way. If you can pull off this last return option, congratulations. You're no longer an intermediate player.

SUCCESS SUMMARY

Here is a quick review of drop-shot fundamentals. Disguise the shot by making it look as much like your normal forehand preparation and swing as possible. Hit with an open racket face and a high-to-low swing. Slow down the speed of the racket head. Use a delicate touch to put

backspin on the ball. Finish with an abbreviated backswing.

In table 8.1, enter your scores for each of the drop-shot drills. If you get 16 out of 37 possible points, go to step 9.

Table 8.1   Scoring Summary

Drop-Shot Drills	
1. Drop-and-hit drop shots	_____ out of 7
2. Drop-shot setups	_____ out of 7
3. Drop-shot points	_____ out of 7
4. Short game	_____ out of 7
5. Drop shots win!	_____ out of 9
TOTAL	_____ *out of 37*

Competing As a Singles Player

The emphasis in this step is not big-picture match strategy, but instead tactical, shot-by-shot decisions. Four factors must be considered. You have little control over the first two, but considerable influence over the others.

The first factor is your opponent. Consider whether your opponent will let you use tactics, meaning he or she won't blow you off the court regardless of your game plan. You can do certain things when the opponent clearly has superior skills, but there are times when tactical planning may be nothing more than an academic exercise.

The second consideration is the environment in which you play. If you are a baseliner forced to play on a slick surface, you may be in trouble. Groundstroke specialists generally play better when the ball bites into the court, bounces up, and slows down. Conversely, servers and volleyers love fast courts and have an advantage playing on a slick surface.

The third factor is your ability to execute shots. It does you no good, for example, to attempt a rush-the-net strategy if you don't have time to practice serves, approach shots, and volleys. Rushing the net does not allow a large margin of error. Many former college players, for instance, find it frustrating to make the adjustment from what they were able to do when practicing six days a week to what they can do when playing league or tournament tennis only one or two days a week.

Finally, tactical tennis demands an understanding of your own game—what you can and can't do realistically. Are you a baseline counter-puncher, an aggressive baseline player, a big hitter, or an all-court player? Are you an advanced player, intermediate player, or beginner? Are you better at singles or doubles? Until you accept who you are and what you are capable (or incapable) of doing, tactics don't help. Some people never get it. They would rather look good losing (this usually means hitting hard) than look bad winning (doing whatever it takes). To choose looking good over winning the game is a poor decision. The key to winning the game is learning to use tactics that are consistent with your true ability.

This chapter is an overview of what to do with groundstrokes, serves, volleys, half volleys, lobs, smashes, and drop shots, all the steps we've covered in this book up to this point. The guidelines presented here are not absolute, but they establish a framework for making sound tactical decisions.

FOREHANDS AND BACKHANDS

Good forehand and backhand groundstrokes can keep you alive in the point, allow you to apply constant pressure, and set things up for winners. Groundstrokes also make opponents move, get tired, make errors, and leave part of the court open for your shots. In singles, groundstrokes are the basic tools that help you build, or set up, points. Here are some suggestions to make your groundstrokes more effective:

- Use a position behind the center of the baseline as home base during a groundstroke rally (figure 9.1).
- Hit most baseline groundstrokes crosscourt and deep.
- During a groundstroke rally, clear the net with room to spare.
- Hit approach shots deep and down the line to set up a good angle on your next shot (figure 9.2).
- Hit approach shots down the middle to neutralize an opponent's speed and reduce the angle of the return.
- Occasionally hit approach shots crosscourt if you can put the ball away.
- Use a shorter backswing against power players.
- Hit with an open stance when you are not planning to follow your shot to the net.
- Hit with an open stance when you are on the run.
- Hit with an open stance when there isn't time to turn and hit.
- When running wide, plant the outside foot and push off back toward your home base.

- When you have no time to recover, go for a down-the-line winner.
- Buy time with a slower slice backhand.
- Develop a slice backhand for the return of serve.
- Develop a slice short backhand to hit at the feet of net rushers.
- Be decisive on passing shots. Don't hesitate.
- Use a slice backhand to keep the ball low against volleyers.
- Use a slice backhand occasionally on approach shots.
- Hit high-bouncing balls to an opponent's backhand.
- Use a shorter backswing against a fast serve.
- Keep the ball low when trying to pass an opponent at the net.
- During a baseline rally, develop a pattern and then break it (figure 9.3).
- To take advantage of your strong forehand (or to protect a weak backhand), run around your backhand (move far enough toward the backhand side) to hit an inside-out forehand.
- Take the ball off the bounce earlier to gain an offensive advantage.
- On power forehands, use less topspin. Hit the ball flat.
- Use topspin to combine power and control.
- When returning a serve, stand near the baseline in the middle of the two extreme angles to which the ball can travel after it is served (figure 9.4).

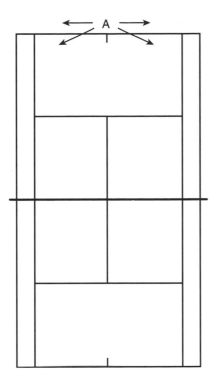

Figure 9.1 Depending on your opponent's position, recover to the center of the baseline between ground-strokes.

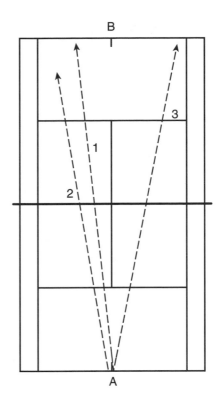

Figure 9.3 Break a groundstroke pattern.

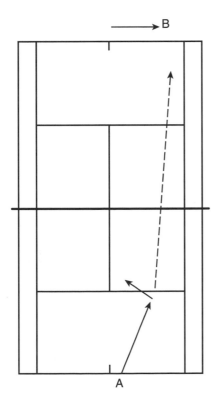

Figure 9.2 Hit approach shots deep and down the line to set up a good angle on your next shot.

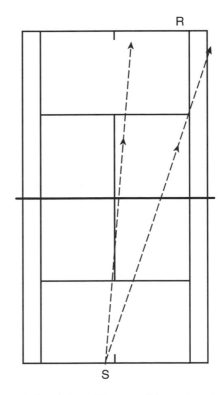

Figure 9.4 Cover the widest possible angles when returning serves.

Approach-Shot Drill. *Approach-Shot Setups*

To practice placing approach shots down the line, have a partner stand at the baseline and feed 10 consecutive balls short and soft to either fore-court side (figure 9.5). Move forward and hit an approach shot deep and down the line. Count the number of approach shots that fall into a corner of your opponent's backcourt.

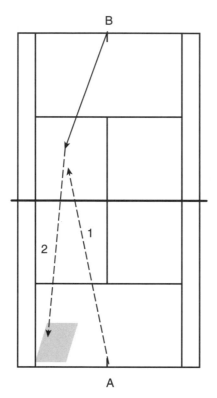

Figure 9.5 Approach-shot setups.

To Increase Difficulty

- Play the point out and score a point only when you win with a volley after the approach shot

To Decrease Difficulty

- Have your partner set up shots only to the forehand or only to the backhand side.

Success Check

- Don't overhit the approach shot.
- Take a shorter backswing if your body weight is moving forward.

Score Your Success

1 to 3 successfully placed approach shots = 1 point

4 to 7 successfully placed approach shots = 3 points

8 to 10 successfully placed approach shots = 5 points

Your score ___

SERVES

The first priority for the serve in singles is to get the ball in play. If you can do this consistently, you can begin to move the ball while varying the pace, location, and spin. If you are not getting at least 60 percent of your first serves in, reduce the pace and/or add more spin. Here's how to get the most out of your serve in singles play:

- Stand near the center of the baseline to serve (figure 9.6).
- Right-handed players should move a step to the right when serving from the deuce court to allow for a serve that pulls the receiver off the court; left-handed players should move a step to the left when serving from the ad court.

- Develop a pre-serve routine.
- Visualize your target.
- Do not waste energy attempting aces on every serve. Pick the best times.
- When you do attempt aces, think middle. The net is lower there, and the court is shorter.
- Use two medium-paced serves rather than one fast serve and one slow one.
- Serve to an opponent's weakness or to an open area.
- Be careful about serving to the receiver's strongest side.
- Use a spin serve to give yourself more time to rush the net after the serve.

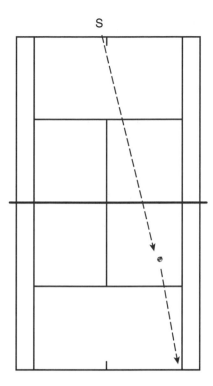

Figure 9.6 Stand near the center of the baseline to serve.

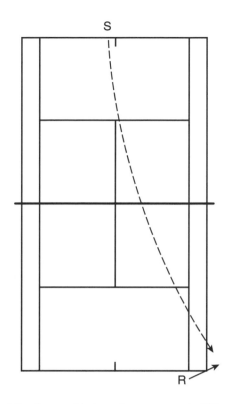

Figure 9.7 Serve wide to pull an opponent off the court.

- Serve wide with spin to pull an opponent off the court (figure 9.7).
- Serve deep into the service court to keep your opponent from attacking.
- Use spin on the serve for greater control.

- Serve conservatively when the score is tied or when you are losing late in a game.
- Serve aggressively at 40-love and 40-15.
- Experiment with a variety of serves (pace, spin, location) during a match.

Serve–Return Drill 1. *Fast Serve–Return*

Return 10 consecutive serves hit by a practice partner. Shorten your backswing, turn your shoulders, and step forward with the opposite foot when possible. Score a point for every serve returned into the singles court and/or score a point for every in serve.

To Increase Difficulty

- Allow the server to serve from within the baseline.
- Stand two steps inside the baseline to return serves.

To Decrease Difficulty

- Ask the server to serve from one step behind the baseline.

- Stand one step behind the baseline to return.

Success Checks

- Rotate shoulders quickly.
- Take a short backswing.

Score Your Success

The server receives 3 points for 1 to 3 in serves, 5 points for 4 to 7 in serves, and 7 points for 8 to 10 in serves.

The receiver earns 3 points for 1 to 3 successful returns, 5 points for 4 to 7 successful returns, and 7 points for 8 to 10 successful returns.

Your score ___

Serve–Return Drill 2. *Serves and Returns*

In this drill, one player practices serving and the other practices returning serves. One player attempts 10 serves, the other 10 consecutive returns. Both players can score points. The server accrues points for serves that are not returned; the receiver earns points for successful returns.

To Increase Difficulty

- For the server, a fault counts as a point lost.
- For the receiver, returns must be deep (back third of the court). Or, the receiver must stand inside the baseline to return a serve.

To Decrease Difficulty

- For the server, attempt only second serves (less pace, more spin).
- For the receiver, serves may be returned within singles or doubles boundaries. Or, a fault counts as a point won.

Success Check

- For the server, visualize your serve before hitting and vary the pace, location, and spin.
- For the receiver, turn the shoulders quickly, and make contact early when the ball is on the rise.

Score Your Success

The server scores 1 point for 1 to 3 serves not returned, 3 points for 4 to 7 serves not returned, and 5 points for 8 to 10 serves not returned.

The receiver earns 1 point for 1 to 3 serves returned, 3 points for 4 to 7 serves returned, and 5 points for 8 to 10 serves returned.

Your score ___

VOLLEYS

Although it is possible to develop a strong singles game relying almost exclusively on groundstrokes, complete players develop the ability to volley from anywhere on the court. They look for openings to get into volleying positions. They force their opponents into positions in which part of the court is left open, and then move in for the kill. Here's how to use volleys to your advantage:

- Stay light on your feet, and take a split step as your opponent gets ready to hit.
- Take a volleying position that bisects the angle of possible returns (figure 9.8).
- Move in closer to the net when you know the return won't be a lob.
- Place volleys into the open part of the court.
- Use a crosscourt volley to return a shot hit down the line (figure 9.9).

- Use a down-the-line volley to return a shot hit crosscourt (figure 9.10).
- When you move to one side to hit a volley, try to move forward at an angle toward the net (figure 9.11).
- After a well-hit volley, move closer to the net for the kill.
- Use the first volley to set yourself up for a winning second volley.
- When in doubt, volley deep to your opponent's weakest side or down the middle.
- Go for safe but deep returns down the line or down the middle on low volleys.
- Go for angled winners that bounce inside the service court on high volleys.
- Expect every shot to be returned after a volley.

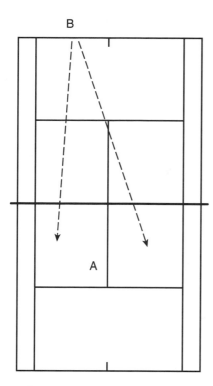

Figure 9.8 Position yourself to bisect the angle of possible returns.

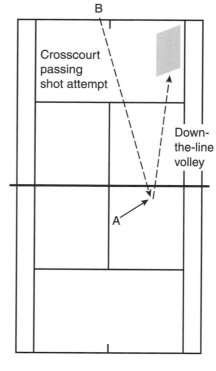

Figure 9.10 Use a down-the-line volley against a crosscourt passing shot.

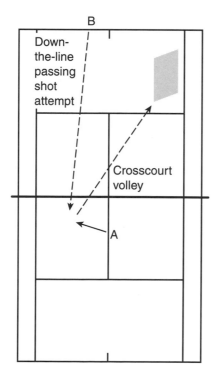

Figure 9.9 Use a crosscourt volley against a down-the-line passing shot.

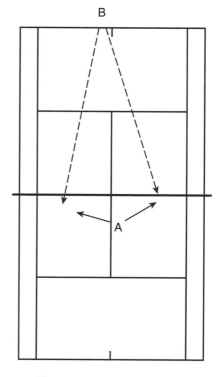

Figure 9.11 Move forward on wide volleys.

Volley Drill 1. *Volley–Pass*

Start in a volley position, and put 10 balls into play so your partner can attempt a passing shot from anywhere on the baseline (figure 9.12). If the attempted passing shot goes shoulder high and down the line, go for the angled crosscourt volley winner. If the ball comes at you low, return it with a volley down the line or down the middle. When the passing shot goes crosscourt, return it with a down-the-line winning volley. The volley–pass is a three-shot drill (setup, passing shot, volley). Count the number of successfully placed volleys.

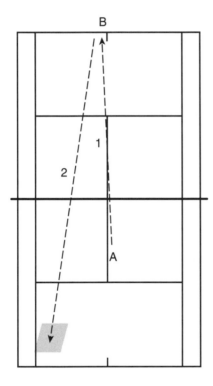

Figure 9.12 Volley–pass.

To Increase Difficulty

- Play the point out and count only the instances when the volleyer wins.

To Decrease Difficulty

- Have the baseline player attempt shots only to the forehand or only to the backhand side.

Success Check

- Stay light on your toes between shots.
- Keep the racket up and in front between volleys.

Score Your Success

1 to 3 successful volleys or wins = 3 points

4 to 7 successful volleys or wins = 5 points

8 to 10 successful volleys or wins = 7 points

Your score ___

Volley Drill 2. *Two-on-One Passing Shots*

Player A begins at the net. Players B and C begin on the opposite baseline. Player A puts 10 consecutive balls into play alternately to B and C (figure 9.13). Player B hits a down-the-line passing shot, which player A returns crosscourt to player C. Player C keeps the rally going with another down-the-line groundstroke. Player A always hits crosscourt volleys. Players B and C always hit down-the-line groundstrokes. This is a difficult team drill that requires controlled strokes from all three players. When a 5-shot sequence is completed, stop the drill and begin again. Track the number of times a 5-shot sequence is completed.

To Increase Difficulty

- Start over every time an error is made.
- Continue the sequence without stopping after five shots.

To Decrease Difficulty

- Pick up the groundstroke–volley sequence from wherever the last error was made.

Success Check

- Move toward the net laterally to cut off passing shots.
- Use the wrist to position the racket for crosscourt returns.

Score Your Success

1 to 3 groundstroke–volley sequences completed = 5 points

4 to 7 groundstroke–volley sequences completed = 7 points

8 to 10 groundstroke–volley sequences completed = 9 points

Your score ___

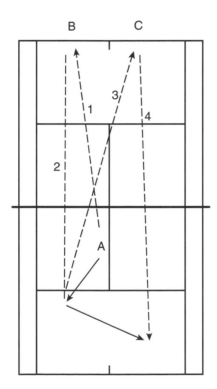

Figure 9.13 Two-on-one passing shots.

LOBS

The lob is one of the most effective shots in singles, especially against very aggressive players and those who have weak smashes. Use the lob often enough to keep your opponent off balance. If it works, use it even more. Here are some tips for making your lob a successful stroke:

- If you make a mistake with a lob, make it deep rather than short (figure 9.14).

- Use the lob more often when your opponent has to look into the sun.

- Hit most defensive lobs crosscourt (figure 9.15).

- Follow good offensive lobs to the net. Stop near the service line.

- Sometimes hit the lob just to make your opponent aware that your lob is a threat.

- When in a defensive position, lob high to buy time.

- Lob low when you are trying to win a point with the shot.

- Lob to the backhand if you can do it without risking an error.

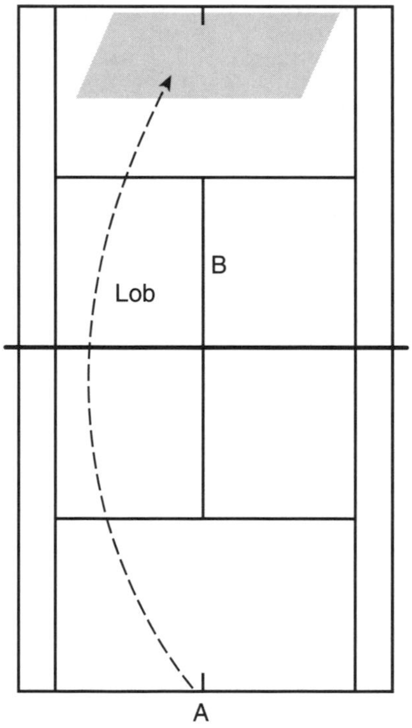

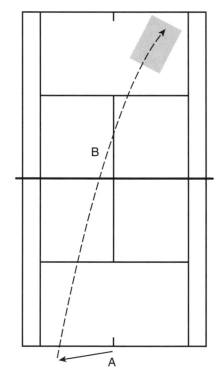

Figure 9.14 Aim for the backcourt on lobs.

Figure 9.15 Hit defensive lobs crosscourt.

Lob Drill. *Approach–Lob*

Begin at the middle of the baseline. Put 10 consecutive balls into play by setting your practice partner up for either a forehand or backhand approach shot deep and down the line (figure 9.16). Return the approach shot with a high crosscourt lob. This is a three-shot drill: setup, approach, lob. If you are the lobber, count the number of times a lob clears your opponent at the net, goes crosscourt, and hits between the service line and the baseline. If you are the approach-shot hitter, count the number of times an approach shot is not successfully returned with a lob.

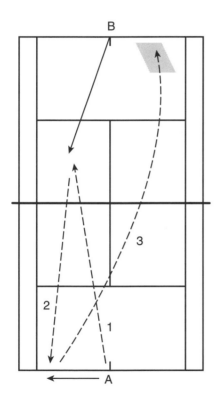

Figure 9.16 Approach–lob.

To Increase Difficulty

- For the player hitting lobs, allow the other player to approach the net and smash short lobs. Or allow your partner to start the drill at midcourt, dropping a ball and driving it deep to either corner.
- For the player hitting the approach shot, count only the approach shots that come within 10 feet of the baseline.

To Decrease Difficulty

- For the player hitting lobs, have your partner hit all 10 approach shots to the same corner. Or score a point for any lob that reaches the backcourt on either side.
- For the player hitting the approach shot, have your partner hit all 10 setups to the same side. Or count any shot that clears the opposite service line.

Success Check

- For the player hitting lobs, take a quick first step and hit the lob crosscourt.
- For the player hitting the approach shot, use underspin on shots that stay low to keep the approach shot low. On shots that bounce high, hit a flatter, harder approach shot.

Score Your Success

The player hitting lobs receives 5 points for 1 to 3 successful lobs, 7 points for 4 to 7 successful lobs, and 9 points for 8 to 10 successful lobs.

The player hitting approach shots earns 5 points for 1 to 3 successful approach shots, 7 points for 4 to 7 successful approach shots, and 9 points for 8 to 10 successful approach shots.

Your score ___

SMASHES

As you develop into a full-court player, the smash can become the shot that closes out the point. If you put yourself in a position to win but cannot close the point, your work will be wasted. Here are tips for hitting an effective smash:

- Hit a smash after the bounce if you can do it without losing your offensive position.

- Hit a smash before the bounce if you will lose your offensive position after the bounce.

- When close to the net, hit smashes flat (without spin).

- When in the backcourt area, use spin to move the ball away from your opponent.

- Change the direction of a second consecutive smash.

- When you are close to the net, hit smashes at an angle (figure 9.17).

- Hit smashes to a corner if you are deep in your backcourt.

- Do not try a put-away smash if you are near the baseline.

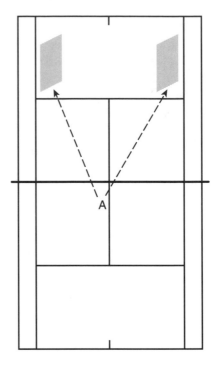

Figure 9.17 Smash at an angle when close to the net.

Smash Drill 1. *Lob–Smash*

The lob–smash drill is similar to the approach–lob drill but with a different kind of pressure setup. Have your partner start from the T and hit 10 forcing shots anywhere deep into your backcourt (figure 9.18). Move quickly to retrieve the shot with a lob while your partner moves to smash your lob if it is short. If your lob is deep, your opponent retreats, allows the ball to bounce, and hits an overhead smash into the open court. Hit three shots, then start over. A successful lob is one that forces your opponent to retreat to smash before or after the bounce. A successful smash is one hit to the open court before or after the bounce.

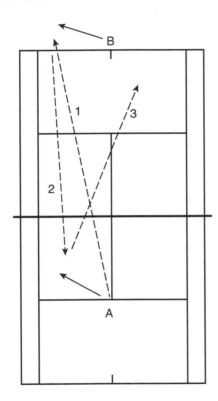

Figure 9.18 Lob-smash.

To Increase Difficulty

- For the player hitting lobs, play the point out and count only the times you win the point.
- For the player hitting smashes, play the point out and count only the times you win the point with the first smash.

To Decrease Difficulty

- For the player hitting lobs, have your partner hit drives only to the forehand or the backhand corner. Or, count any shot retrieved and returned anywhere in the singles court.
- For the player hitting smashes, play the point out and count only the times you win the point with a subsequent shot.

Success Check

- For the player hitting lobs, use a down-to-up racket motion and hit the lob crosscourt to reduce your opponent's angle of return
- For the player hitting smashes, smash to the open court and allow a margin of error. Don't aim for the lines.

Score Your Success

The player hitting lobs scores 5 points for 1 to 3 successful lobs, 7 points for 4 to 7 successful lobs, and 9 points for 8 to 10 successful lobs.

The player hitting smashes earns 5 points for 1 to 3 winning smashes, 7 points for 4 to 7 winning smashes, and 9 points for 8 to 10 winning smashes.

Your score ___

Smash Drill 2. *Serve–Return–Attack*

This drill combines several strokes and simulates play at a relatively high level. Put the ball into play 10 times with a serve (figure 9.19). The receiver returns deliberately short into your forecourt. Move forward and drive the ball deep into the backcourt. Depending on how good your approach shot is, your partner either attempts a passing shot or puts up a lob. After that, anything goes. Play 10 total points before changing roles.

To Increase Difficulty

- The point is lost immediately with serves that are out.

To Decrease Difficulty

- Both players hit controlled shots until the lob, then the point begins.

Success Check

- Stay light on your feet.
- Bisect the opponent's angle of return.

Score Your Success

1 to 3 points won = 5 points

4 to 7 points won = 7 points

8 to 10 points won = 9 points

Your score ___

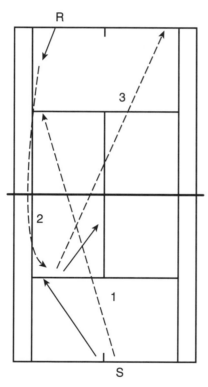

Figure 9.19   Serve–return–attack.

DROP SHOTS

Use the drop shot often enough to keep your opponent honest. Let the other player know you can and will try this shot. Don't overuse this shot, and follow these suggestions regarding drop-shot tactics:

- Hit drop shots from the forecourt area.
- Use drop shots against slow-moving players.

- Use drop shots against players who are in poor physical condition.
- Do not try drop shots when a strong wind is at your back.
- Do not try drop shots against players who can cover the court well.

Drop-Shot Drill. *Drop Shot–Lob*

Test your strokes and court movement with the drop-shot–lob drill. Start at the forecourt T and put 10 balls into play with a drop shot (figure 9.20). Your practice opponent moves forward from the baseline and returns your drop shot with a counter drop shot. You respond to that drop shot with a lob and the contest is on. Play the point out.

To Increase Difficulty

- Both players start from the baseline and hit until an opportunity for a drop shot arises.

To Decrease Difficulty

- Both players start from opposing Ts.

Success Check

- Take a quick first step to the ball.
- Use a delicate touch on drop shots and lobs.

Score Your Success

1 to 3 points won = 5 points

4 to 7 points won = 7 points

8 to 10 points won = 9 points

Your score ___

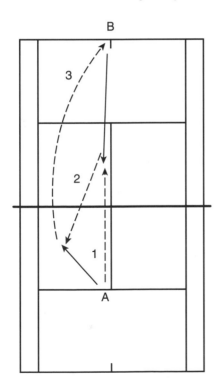

Figure 9.20 Drop shot–lob.

GENERAL TACTICS

Regardless of the stroke being used in singles play, keep in mind some general guidelines as you develop a game plan. Don't waste time worrying about the end result. Concentrate on the next shot and the next point. If you find yourself playing "loose" points, plan the first three shots of each point. Consider these strategies:

- If you win the spin of the racket, choose to serve first if you have a good serve.

- If your opponent chooses to serve first, choose the side against the wind for the first game.

- Use a variety of shots in the first two games to show an opponent what you might do at any time.

- Hit the simplest shot that will win the point.

- Use your best shot in crucial situations.

- Anticipate your opponent's best shot in crucial situations.

- In pressure situations, play the ball instead of your opponent.

- If you are having problems adjusting to a surface, go to the net more often.

- Slow down the match if you are losing in a hurry.

- Aim for general target areas rather than lines.

- Do not try risky shots on critical points. Take chances on points you can afford to lose.

- When losing, check stroke fundamentals before changing strategy or tactics.

ARE YOU PLAYING NOT TO LOSE?

In Las Vegas a very good tennis player who was an occasional, small-time bettor challenged a professional gambler, but mediocre tennis player, to a match.

"How much do you want to play for?" asked the gambler.

"One hundred dollars a set, two out of three sets," replied the tournament player.

"No, I won't do that," countered the gambler, "but I'll play you for a thousand dollars a set."

The skilled player was shaken, but he agreed. He lost in straight sets—6-1, 6-2—and the gambler took his $2,000 and went home.

Why did the better player lose? Because when there was something at stake, in this case $2,000 of his money, the better player played merely not to lose instead of playing to win. It is a phenomenon often seen in both individual and team sports. For a variety of reasons, most of which have nothing to do with money, athletes in positions to win become conservative, tentative, scared, negative, or perhaps all of the above.

"This type of athlete begins to lose focus, which is replaced by inhibitions that weren't there before," explains Evan Brody, PhD, a sport psychophysiologist in Olney, Maryland. "Then a process sets in that interferes with thinking as well as the ability to execute physical actions. When a person starts having second thoughts instead of doing what he or she has been trained to do, it shows up as an inability to perform efficient and flowing types of movement."

"The level of interference can slightly throw you off your game," continues Brody, "or it can become debilitating. It happens every once in a while to professional tennis players, golfers, and baseball players. Their information processors don't work efficiently, and that carries over to the ability of the body to execute a skill."

David Yukelson, PhD, a sport psychologist at Penn State, describes playing not to lose this way: "A team is way ahead in basketball and decides to take time off of the clock. Then the defensive intensity of the opponent picks up, the lead is cut in half, and that cognitive-physiological thing in the body says, 'uh-oh.' At that point, the team becomes timid, indecisive, and playing not to make a mistake. There is a momentum change that is difficult to stop."

So what can you do about it? "At the planning and practice stage with individual athletes," says Brody, "it's a matter of setting short-term and midterm goals instead of always thinking about the long-term goal of winning. You have to look at what it takes, mentally laying out a game plan. That, in turn, takes skill to play the sport and ability to deal with adversity during events. Both take time to develop."

Brody thinks that the battle may already be lost in some athletes when inhibitory processes start to surface. It may be related to personality, or it may depend on how much training has been devoted to switching gears, when necessary. If tennis players haven't been trained to regain their composure, figure out what is happening, and refocus on what it takes to get back on track, they are not likely to succeed.

Preliminary research shows that in experienced marksmen less communication takes place between the frontal lobe of the brain (where the cognitive process is centered) and the motor cortex than what occurs in inexperienced performers. With more experience, the motor cortex doesn't have to tell your body to do something in a certain way. It just happens. That is why athletes put their bodies into positions time after time to get a feel for what they are doing. The more they do it, the more a skill pattern is laid down in the motor cortex. People call it muscle memory, but the memory is actually happening in the brain. And this type of automatic, nonthinking response doesn't "just happen" in novices.

Brody suggests that when outside, irrelevant, and negative thoughts start getting in the way of our performance, we should try for a solution that involves only one or two elements. "In a sport like tennis that involves a swing, don't go back and think about the way your total swing looked when things were going well. Instead, find a swing that is comfortable for the moment, even if it is not technically sound. Come up with some kind of positive cue or change that is simple enough to help you regain focus."

Positive verbal cues, either from a coach or in the form of self-talk, work for some athletes in all sports. For example, Jimmy Johnson, the former coach of the Cowboys and Dolphins, is said to have told his running backs, "Protect the ball," instead of advising, "Don't fumble." A tennis coach might say, "Hit out on your forehand and backhand," instead of, "Don't be timid on your groundstrokes."

Yukelson thinks that preparing to go all out all the time, while remaining confident and aggressive, is the key to avoiding the "playing not to lose" syndrome. "When you recognize signs of apprehensiveness in your effort or feel a momentum shift," he advises, "take a mental time-out. Step back, refocus, and then close the deal."

"Be a momentum maker," concludes Yukelson. "Take it to your opponent rather than waiting for something bad to happen. Compete with controlled aggressiveness for the duration of a match."

SUCCESS SUMMARY

Try to keep your singles strategy simple. The idea is to get the ball over the net and into the court one time more than your opponent. You have two ways to accomplish this: Keep the ball in play, and hit the ball so your opponent can't return it. In that sense, singles tactics are more about common sense than anything else.

Decide who you are on the tennis court. If your strength is at the baseline because you can counter with forehand and backhand groundstrokes, do it. Don't pretend you are a power player who can blast opponents off the court. Spend most of your time at the baseline, but work to become a better all-court player. If you can use your physical strength and speed to

hit forcing shots such as volleys and smashes, do so. But use some of your practice time to develop the consistency and patience to also become effective at the baseline. You may even become experienced enough to use a variety of styles.

Playing styles are not good or bad. They simply either work for you or they don't. The important thing is to recognize your talents and your limitations. Then get busy becoming a better player, whatever your style.

In table 9.1, enter your scores for each of the singles strategy drills. If you score 30 out of 69 possible points, you're doing great. Even if you don't, go to step 10, doubles strategy, anyway.

Table 9.1   Scoring Summary

Approach-Shot Drill	
1. Approach-shot setups	_____ out of 5
Serve–Return Drills	
1. Fast serve–return	_____ out of 7
2. Serves and returns	_____ out of 5
Volley Drills	
1. Volley–pass	_____ out of 7
2. Two-on-one passing shots	_____ out of 9
Lob Drill	
1. Approach–lob	_____ out of 9
Smash Drills	
1. Lob–smash	_____ out of 9
2. Serve–return–attack	_____ out of 9
Drop-Shot Drill	
1. Drop shot–lob	_____ out of 9
TOTAL	_____ ***out of 69***

Playing As a Doubles Team

Most players begin to excel at doubles long after they have achieved success in singles. Speed, power, and endurance become less important than court position, anticipation, and shot selection. Two good heads win as many points as four good legs. Winning doubles demands "thinking tennis," and the strategies and tactics presented in this step will enable you to elevate the mental level of your game.

POACHING

When the server's partner at the net moves across the court to cut off a crosscourt service return with a volley, it's called *poaching*. Poaching is a very effective maneuver for winning points, intimidating the receiver, and keeping the other team off balance. But it is a skill that takes time to perfect in terms of movement, technique, timing, and communication. Poaching has to be used to interject an element of surprise; it should not be something so obvious that the opponents can anticipate what is about to happen.

The movement to poach has to be quick, deliberate, and at an angle in the direction of the net (for power), not parallel to it or in a line away from it. The technique for the volley used to poach is no different from any other volley. Use a short backswing, make contact with the

ball as early as possible, and go for a winner. If you don't go for a winner, you will put your team in a difficult court position to play out the point. If you are not a strong volleyer, don't poach very often—just enough to pose a threat.

Timing is crucial. Make your move at exactly the moment when the receiver has committed to making a crosscourt return. Move too early, and you give away the surprise element. Do it too late, and you can't catch up to the ball.

Communication between partners is the element that requires time to develop. Inexperienced doubles players and those not accustomed to each other should poach rarely—only when they can afford to lose the point. Some teams use behind-the-back hand signals to indicate an upcoming poach. A closed fist means no poach; an open hand indicates a poach on the next serve. Teams that have played together for a long time don't necessarily need signals. They have a feel for each other, what needs to happen, and when it should happen. If you're not sure about whether a poach is the right thing to do in a critical situation, talk to your partner about it. But don't go for a poach on every point.

GROUNDSTROKES AND SERVICE RETURNS

Groundstrokes are necessary, but effective doubles players win with serves, volleys, and smashes. Forehands and backhands from the baseline are a means of getting into position to win points with more forceful shots. Consider these strategies:

- Return serves from a point approximately where the baseline meets the singles sideline (figure 10.1). The server stands behind the baseline a few feet from the singles sideline. The server's partner stands 8 to 10 feet from the net inside the singles sideline. The receiver's partner stands on the service line between the center service line and the singles sideline.
- Move in against players with weak serves.
- If the server remains on the baseline after the serve, return the ball deep and crosscourt; then follow your shot to the net (figure 10.2).
- If the server comes to the net after the serve, return the ball crosscourt and to the server's feet (figure 10.3).
- When you try to pass the server's partner at the net, aim for the singles sideline.
- Test the server's partner early in a match.
- Attempt to pass the net player occasionally, even if you lose the point.
- When your partner is forced out of position, shift to cover the open court (figure 10.4).

- Let the player on your team with the forehand position take most shots that come down the middle.
- When in doubt and your opponents are at the net, hit low and down the middle.
- Don't rely on groundstrokes to win in doubles.
- Protect the middle.
- Force the action.

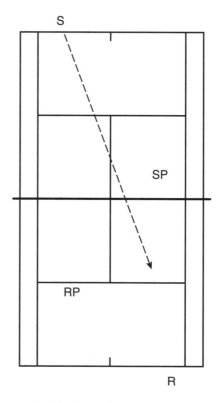

Figure 10.1 Positioning at the start of a doubles point.

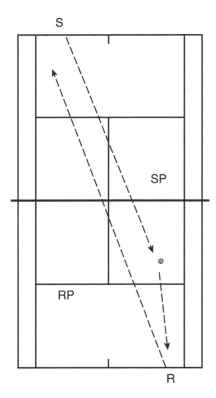

Figure 10.2 Approaching the net after a serve return.

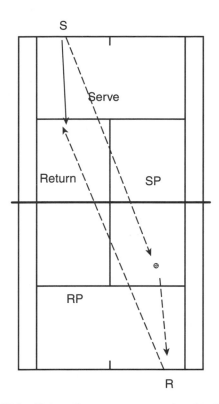

Figure 10.3 Return the serve crosscourt and to the server's feet.

Figure 10.4 Covering the open court.

Serve–Return Drill. *Serve–Crosscourt Return*

Play to 10 points. One player serves all points. If the server stays at the baseline, the receiver sends the ball crosscourt and deep. If the server comes to the net, the receiver sends the ball crosscourt but short so that the server has to attempt a low shot. Do not poach on the first return. Play the point out.

To Increase Difficulty

- Allow the server's partner to poach (when appropriate) after the serve.

To Decrease Difficulty

- The point doesn't begin until the third shot.
- The server stays back after serving.

Success Check

- Take a short backswing on return of serve.
- Return deep if server stays back; return shallow if server rushes.

Score Your Success

1 to 3 points won = 3 points

4 to 7 points won = 5 points

8 to 10 points won = 7 points

Your score ___

Groundstroke Drill. *Attacking Groundstrokes*

Players A and B play against players C and D. Players exchange continuous groundstrokes from the baseline. Put 10 balls into play, alternating first shots from team to team. As soon as either team hits a shot that falls into the opponents' service court area, the opponents return the ball deep and move forward to volleying positions near the net (figure 10.5). Play the point out.

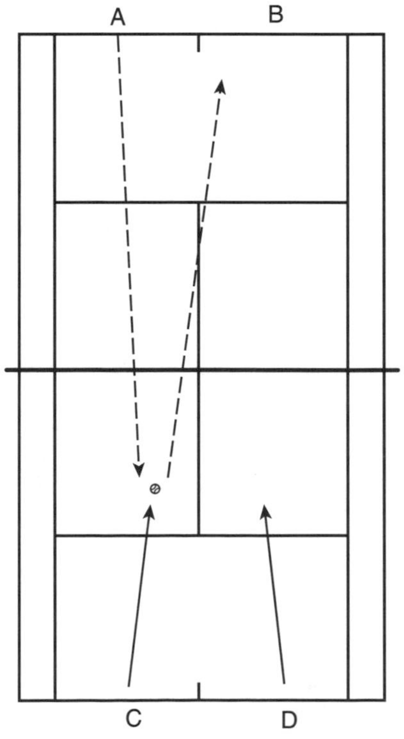

To Increase Difficulty

- Keep the ball in play four shots before the point begins.

To Decrease Difficulty

- Designate only one team to be the attackers.

Success Check

- Be aggressive.
- Hit groundstrokes high and deep.

Score Your Success

1 to 3 points won = 3 points

4 to 7 points won = 5 points

8 to 10 points won = 7 points

Your score ___

Figure 10.5   Attacking groundstrokes.

SERVES

Placing the ball in a specific location with the serve sets up the whole point. If you can place your serve, you can control what happens instead of reacting to what your opponents choose to do. Once you figure out where the other players are weak or which spots on the court they leave open, you have to be able to hit those spots. Placing your serve effectively is a relatively sophisticated skill that requires a lot of practice. The main objective still is to get the ball into play, but putting it in the right places will make things easier for you and your partner. Here's how to get the most from your serve:

- Let the best server begin serving each set.
- Stand approximately halfway between the center mark and the doubles sidelines to serve (see figure 10.1, page 120).
- Serve deep to the backhand or to an open area.
- Serve most balls down the middle.
- Serve wide to a right-handed player's backhand in the ad (left) court to pull your opponent off the court.
- Serve wide to a left-handed player's backhand in the deuce (right) court to pull your opponent off the court.
- Serve directly at a receiver who has a big backswing.

- Add more spin on serves to give yourself time to get to the net.
- Serve down the middle if your partner is good at poaching (figure 10.6).

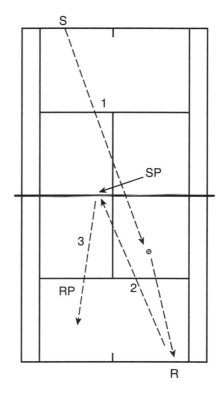

Figure 10.6 Serve, return, and poach.

123

Serve Drill 1. *Serve–Rush–Volley*

The server serves 10 times and gets into position to hit volleys from midcourt or closer (figure 10.7). The receiver returns the ball crosscourt and the point is on.

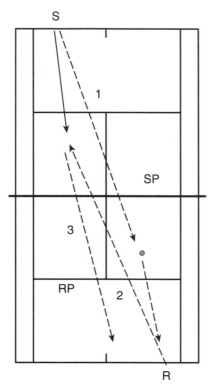

Figure 10.7 Serve–rush–volley.

To Increase Difficulty

- Only count points when the serving team wins on its second shot.

To Decrease Difficulty

- The server gets two chances on each serve.

Success Check

- Serve deep.
- Take a split step on the way to the net.

Score Your Success

1 to 3 points won by serving team = 3 points

4 to 7 points won by serving team = 5 points

8 to 10 points won by serving team = 7 points

Your score ___

Serve Drill 2. *Serve–Return–Poach*

The server serves 10 times. The receiver sends the ball back. The server's partner poaches and volleys to the open court or to the receiver's partner at the opposite service line. For the sake of this drill, the receiver must return crosscourt. Play the point out.

To Increase Difficulty

- The server's partner is not required to return crosscourt.
- Serves must strike the court within six feet of the service line. Mark the court with chalk.

To Decrease Difficulty

- Allow the server two attempts on each serve.

- The receiver sets up the poacher with a head-high, medium-paced crosscourt return.

Success Check

- Serve deep and down the middle.
- Poach in a diagonal toward the net.

Score Your Success

1 to 3 points won = 3 points

4 to 7 points won = 5 points

8 to 10 points won = 7 points

Your score ___

VOLLEYS

Good doubles players can serve to specific spots and follow those serves with volleys. The team that gets to the net first controls the outcome of the point. They may not win the point, but they decide who does. If you can chip the ball short or drive it crosscourt and deep on serve returns, follow your shot to the net to get into a volleying position. Keep these volleying strategies in mind:

- When your partner is serving, stand about 8 to 12 feet from the net and two to three steps inside the singles sideline (see figure 10.1, page 120).

- When your partner serves wide, shift slightly toward the alley.

- When your partner is serving, protect your side of the court, take weak shots down the middle, and smash any lobs hit to your side of the court unless your partner calls for the shot.

- In quick exchanges at the net, the last player to hit a shot should take the next shot if it comes down the middle.

- When you poach, go for a winner.

- Move diagonally toward the net for a poach instead of parallel to it (figure 10.8).

- Poach occasionally, even if you lose the point.

- Poach more often when your partner is serving well.

- Poach more often when your partner serves down the middle than when the serve goes wide.

- Poach less often if your partner has a good volley.

- Fake the poach at times.

- During rallies, look at the racket faces of your opponents.

- Stand farther from the net against players who lob frequently.

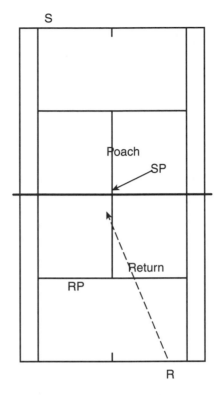

Figure 10.8 Poach diagonally toward the net to cut off the return of serve.

- Play closer to the net against players who seldom lob.

- Retreat quickly, then take a defensive position when your opponents are set up for a smash.

- Stand farther from the net if your partner's serve is weak.

- Shift slightly with every shot to cover the open court.

- Watch your opponents, not your partner, when your partner is returning a serve and during rallies.

- Change sides and fall back to the service line when an opponent lobs over your head.

- Play farther from the net than usual if you are a stronger player than your partner (to occupy more court space).

125

Volley Drill 1. *Continuous Volleys*

Players A, B, C, and D exchange volleys in sequence (A to C to B to D) from positions near the service line (figure 10.9). Put 10 consecutive balls by any player into play. After the third volley, the point is on; and any shot, anywhere, is legal. Score a point for your team with each winning volley.

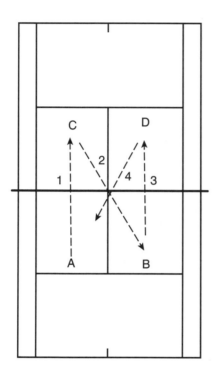

Figure 10.9 Continuous volleys.

To Increase Difficulty

- Competition starts after the fourth volley in the sequence.

To Decrease Difficulty

- Don't follow the initial sequence. The point begins with the third shot.
- Follow the sequence, and count the number of consecutive hits by both teams.

Success Check

- Keep the racket up.
- Move forward to finish the point.
- Go for the open area on the winner.

Score Your Success

1 to 3 points won = 3 points

4 to 7 points won = 5 points

8 to 10 points won = 7 points

Your score ___

Volley Drill 2. *Two-Up, Two-Back Volleys*

Play to 10 points. Either team can put the ball into play. Players A and B start at the baseline and hit groundstrokes to players C and D. Players C and D take positions at the net and hit volleys (figure 10.10). The point begins after the third shot. Once the real point is on, both teams try to force a mistake by their opponents. If the volleyers return a ball that lands softly in the forecourt, both players A and B move in for the kill. If players A and B return a volley with a soft floater, players C and D should be ready to move even closer to the net for the put-away volley or smash.

To Increase Difficulty

- The point begins after the fourth shot.

To Decrease Difficulty

- Designate one team only to keep the ball in play. Allow no forcing shots.

Success Check

- Return low shots with deep, down-the-middle volleys.
- Cut off high shots with angled volleys.
- Protect against the lob.

Score Your Success

1 to 3 points won = 3 points

4 to 7 points won = 5 points

8 to 10 points won = 7 points

Your score ___

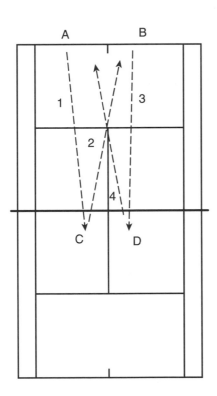

Figure 10.10   Two-up, two-back volleys.

LOBS

Although the lob is not a primary weapon in doubles, it should certainly be an integral part of a doubles team's offensive and defensive array of shots. Having a variety of shots and knowing when to use them can offset the power game of aggressive doubles opponents. Here are some tactics to consider on the lob:

- Use the offensive lob if the net player poaches often.
- When in doubt, lob deep and down the center of the court.
- Lob low on offense and high on defense.
- Lob over the player closer to the net, then follow your lob toward the net.

Lob Drill. *Serve–Lob*

Play 10 consecutive points with the same player serving (figure 10.11). The server serves. The receiver sends a lob over the server's partner at the net. The server's partner smashes the ball or moves to cover the other side of the court. The server has to get the serve deep into the service court. The receiver has to disguise the lob until the last second before contact with the ball. The receiver should also follow a successful lob by moving in to the service line or closer for the next shot. The point starts with the serve.

To Increase Difficulty

- The player at the net stands farther back to take away open court space.

To Decrease Difficulty

- The player at the net starts the point as close to the net as possible to allow more open court space.

Success Check

- Send first lob low over the server's partner.
- Follow the lob to a service-line position or closer.

Score Your Success

1 to 3 points won = 3 points

4 to 7 points won = 5 points

8 to 10 points won = 7 points

Your score ___

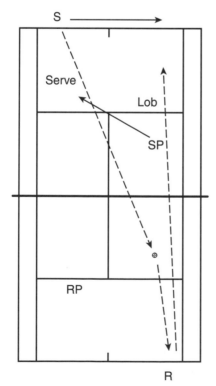

Figure 10.11 Serve–lob.

SMASHES AND DROP SHOTS

The smash in doubles is not just important, it is essential. If the other team figures out that either you or your partner cannot hit winning smashes, watch out! Because every serving point begins with one player at the net, that person will be tested early to see what happens on a lob to that side. Also, because the idea in doubles is to take away the net from the other team as early as possible, you must be able to finish the point with a winning smash. Here's how to hit winning smashes:

- Smash at an angle to open up the opponent's court.
- Smash down the middle to create confusion between your opponents.
- Let the partner with the strongest smash take overheads down the middle.
- Hit smashes at players in weak positions.

Using drop shots in doubles is not usually a good idea. If you try a drop shot, wait until your opponents are pushed deep and out of position; then hit to the side of the slowest player.

Smash Drill. *Two-Up, Two-Back Smashes*

Play to 10 points. Either player A or player B puts 10 balls into play from the baseline using lobs (figure 10.12). At the net, either player C or D hits an overhead smash and the point begins.

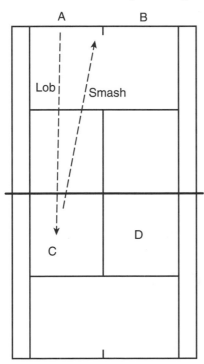

Figure 10.12 Two-up, two-back smashes.

To Increase Difficulty

- Hit setup lobs deeper to start the drill.

To Decrease Difficulty

- Hit lobs shorter and lower on setups.

Success Check

- Make a quick turn and retreat.
- Hold the racket in a cocked position. Stay away from full swings.
- Use down-the-middle smashes to create confusion.
- Hit wide smashes to open the court.

Score Your Success

1 to 3 points won = 3 points

4 to 7 points won = 5 points

8 to 10 points won = 7 points

Your score ____

MIXED DOUBLES

The idea behind social mixed doubles is for everyone to have a good time, to get into the action, and to come away from a match in good physical and emotional health. Therefore, recreational mixed doubles has some unwritten rules. Those rules are mostly don'ts involving how to play against a weaker opponent, such as the following:

- Don't deliberately smash a setup directly at the weaker partner.
- Don't hit too many shots at the weaker partner.
- Don't try to intimidate the weaker player on a team by hitting hard shots at that player, especially when he or she is at the net.

In tournament competition, these rules do not apply. Competitive mixed doubles should be played exactly like men's and women's doubles. Serves should be hit with the velocity and to the place in the service court most likely to produce a winning point, regardless of the receiver's gender. Shots should be directed to the weaker player if the situation calls for it. Each player should cover his or her side of the court. One partner should not cut in front of the other unless percentage tennis (hitting the safest, most effective shot in a given situation) would dictate this tactic. If one player poaches too often or hogs groundstrokes, that player weakens the team's position by leaving part of the court open for the return. This behavior is also demeaning to the player's partner.

Given the general level of men's and women's tennis, playing mixed doubles probably means that the team with the stronger woman will win. This is especially true if the woman on the team can play well at the net. In the past, women have been hesitant about developing a net game, but that has changed.

Positioning in mixed doubles should depend on which side of the court each partner can play best. Some people believe that the crucial points are played on the ad court and that the stronger partner should play on that side when the other team serves. Even if this theory is true, the advantage of having each player play from the side on which he or she is most effective and comfortable outweighs the crucial point theory.

Because mixed doubles usually has the least priority in practice and playing time, use as many shots as you can that create teamwork problems between opposing partners. Moving the ball around the court as much as possible is a good way to manipulate the other team. Lobs are especially effective because one player has to give way to the other, or the partners have to change positions on the court before hitting. Drop shots are usually not a good idea, but they work in mixed doubles to move opponents out of position and open an area for a winning shot.

Finally, make the opposing mixed doubles team do what its members do not want to do. If either player is shy about playing the net, make that player come to the net by hitting short shots. If the team is very aggressive and likes coming to the net, use the lob to keep the partners off balance. If one partner wants to dominate, make that player get out of position to do it. If the partners are not used to playing together, hit a lot of shots down the middle.

WHO'S YOUR PARTNER?

Who you play with can be as important as how well you play. Chemistry, compatibility, and complementing each other's games make for successful, long-lasting teams (and friendships). Consider these suggestions when you have a choice of doubles partners:

- Don't assume that a good singles player is a good doubles player.
- Play with someone you like.
- Play with someone who does not criticize you after a bad shot.

- Play with someone whose strengths compensate for your weaknesses.
- Accept your role as part of a team. Don't try to dominate the match.
- Look for a left-handed player–right-handed player combination.
- Play the left-handed player in the ad court and the right-handed player in the deuce court for effective crosscourt returns.

- Play the left-handed player in the deuce court and the right-handed player in the ad court for down-the-middle coverage.
- Communicate with your partner often.
- Be more aggressive than normal if your partner is a weaker player.
- Fall back to the baseline when your partner is having trouble returning a serve.
- Unless you play regularly with the same partner, learn to play the left and right sides when receiving serves.

WHEN OVERCONFIDENCE MEETS REALITY

The best doubles team doesn't always win. Judging opponents on the basis of their strokes, age, or appearance is a big mistake that often leads to overconfidence. And once the overconfidence train starts rolling, it's hard to stop.

"Sooner or later, overconfidence meets reality and a correction occurs," says John Heil, DA, and sport psychologist, of Roanoke, Virginia, sounding more like a stock market analyst than a sport psychologist when discussing the problem of overconfidence in athletes. "The sooner that reality check happens, the less damage there will be."

Sport psychologists describe self-confidence as a person's (or team's) belief that he or she (or they) can perform difficult tasks in certain conditions. Overconfidence develops when the team misjudges those conditions. The partners tend to pay less attention to detail, ignore critical information, and lack focus both in preparation and during competition. All of these factors lead to flaws in judgment that set the stage for losing to an underdog.

Overconfidence surfaces in at least three ways, none of them very pretty. The first is to look past a supposedly lesser opponent. An unfocused or a less-than-serious approach to practice is a recipe for disaster, regardless of who is next on the schedule. Preparing for opponents who should allow for an easy win can be more difficult than getting ready for top-flight competition. It is a perfectly natural response to take for granted a win over players

who are smaller, slower, weaker, less skilled, or who have a poor record. It is also possible to lose to a weaker team, and that's why weaker teams stay in the game.

Heil describes a second way the overconfidence problem plays out: "The athlete or team who underestimates an opponent and gets behind in a contest may have a very difficult time coming back. A lesser competitor or team can be completely outplayed, but [that team] keeps the match close, gets lucky near the end of the game, and wins."

The third risk of overconfidence is allowing the lesser opponent to hang around long enough during a game or race to gain confidence. Confucius may have said, "Overconfidence breeds carelessness." The sport psychology version of that quote is, "Overconfidence can quickly lead to a reversal in attitudes, in which the favorite quickly loses momentum and the opponent gains confidence at a fast pace."

In sports events, there comes a point at which it does not matter who is best on paper. During the last two minutes of a close basketball game, during the last set of a close tennis match, or in a sudden-death playoff in other sports, it really doesn't matter who is supposed to be better. It's who makes a play, gets a break, is in the best condition, or wants to win the most. Talent does not guarantee victory.

"Overconfidence is often the result of athletes being unaccountable for their shortcomings," says Heil. "Then they think they can bypass the reality check. Those who have exaggerated opinions of themselves—and it happens often among tennis players—look for alternate explanations when things don't work out. They blame coaches, referees, linespeople, teammates, playing conditions, or whatever shifts the excuse for underperforming to someone else. That is one of the reasons some players bounce from coach to coach or partner or to partner when things go wrong."

"The solution," says Heil, "is to prepare, play in the moment, and accept responsibility for your actions. Deal with the situation in front of you, not one you remember or have read about in the paper or take for granted." As they say on Wall Street, "Past performance does not guarantee results." When playing against weaker opponents you had better be a day-trader instead of standing pat.

SUCCESS SUMMARY

The points in doubles matches begin with very structured shots: Serve into the backhand or open court, return crosscourt, approach the net as soon as possible, and so on. Then things get crazy. With four players, wider boundaries, and inviting angles, that structure dissolves into wild, long, unpredictable, and exciting points.

Remember these doubles fundamentals: deep serves; crosscourt returns (most of the time); and

crisp, aggressive volleys. Hit groundstrokes down the middle when opponents are at the net. Hit smashes down the middle to create confusion. Hit smashes wide to open up the court.

Enter your scores for each of the doubles drills in table 10.1. The goal is to score at least 28 out of 56 possible points.

Table 10.1   Scoring Summary

Serve–Return Drill	
1. Serve–crosscourt return	_____ out of 7
Groundstroke Drill	
1. Attacking groundstrokes	_____ out of 7
Serve Drills	
1. Serve–rush–volley	_____ out of 7
2. Serve–return–poach	_____ out of 7
Volley Drills	
1. Continuous volleys	_____ out of 7
2. Two-up, two-back volleys	_____ out of 7
Lob Drill	
1. Serve–lob	_____ out of 7
Smash Drill	
1. Two-up, two-back smashes	_____ out of 7
TOTAL	_____ ***out of 56***

Preparing for the Match

Most matches have their ups and downs. Even when you are winning, expect the other player to make a run at you sooner or later. Before a match begins, set realistic goals. Once the match starts, avoid falling into predictable patterns of play. Play the ball, not the opponent. Check your fundamentals before changing your mental approach. Maintain focus regardless of what happens across the net.

All opponents are not created equal. They bring different abilities and playing styles to their matches. Your ability to manage these variables will make a difference in whether you win or lose. The first part of this chapter contains some suggestions to help you make the necessary adjustments to play different opponents.

Once you have successfully worked through steps on strokes, match strategy, and situational tactics to use against different kinds of players, the last challenge is learning to adjust to playing conditions such as fast courts, slow courts, wind, hot weather, cold weather, and excessive noise. The second part of this chapter includes advice on adjusting to these conditions so that you can take your game to the next level.

PLAYING AGAINST YOURSELF

Although outside distractions are many, most concentration problems arise in our own minds. We let our thoughts drift. We think about our families, jobs, or studies. We worry about people seeing us make a bad shot. And we think about a thousand other things. Start by reducing extraneous thoughts not related to the game, and then work on ways to further sharpen your focus.

It is impossible to cut out all nontennis thoughts, but at least try to eliminate the most obvious ones. Play one point at a time. Your opponent is not likely to hit any shot that you have not at least seen before this match. In fact, you have probably returned every type of shot he or she has to offer. All the other player can do is hit a tennis ball. You might see some shots more often or in different situations, but there aren't that many surprises out there. If you are overmatched, try to win points. If you can win a few points, you can win a game. If you can win a game, you can probably win some more.

Before trying to reach a higher level of concentration, be sure you want to. Millions of players just want to go out, hit the ball, have a good time, and not worry about directing their total attention to the game being played. After all, it's fun to talk with friends, be out-of-doors, watch others play, and relax. But if you want to play really good tennis, you don't have the luxury of thinking about all these other things.

With so many things not to think about, what should you think about during a match? People can only direct their attention to one thing at a time, so establish a priority of thoughts. At the top of the list is the tennis ball. "Keep your eye on the ball" should be more than a platitude. If you are serving, try to watch the ball until it leaves your racket strings. If you are receiving the serve, focus on the ball while it is still in the tossing hand of the server. Follow it with your eyes from the toss to the point of contact, across the net, and into your racket.

Don't worry about whether the serve is in or out until after you have swung at the ball. There is no penalty for calling a shot out after you hit it. Continue concentrating on the ball throughout the point. Watch it when your opponent is preparing to hit and when you are hitting.

The second concentration priority is your opponent. As the ball leaves your racket, you will have a second or two to watch where your opponent is on the court and how he or she is going to hit the next shot. Pay special attention to the other player's racket face. If you look at anything else other than the racket and the ball, you can be faked out of position. Immediately

after the ball is hit to you, be aware of where your opponent is moving on the court.

In this situation, your mind will have to move rapidly back and forth between priority items. You have to be observant enough to know whether the other player is coming to the net, returning to the center of the baseline, or moving to one side of the court. Within a split-second, your attention must again return to the ball.

The third priority on your think list is the method of hitting the ball. You are much better off if you move into the proper position automatically rather than having to think about it. You are preparing for a stroke at the same time you are trying to concentrate on the ball; you cannot think about both simultaneously. If your strokes are practiced to the point of thoughtless perfection, you can devote full attention to the ball.

As if trying to direct your attention to the ball, your opponent, and your own form is not enough, other factors are worthy of your attention. The score in the game, the set score, the weather, your physical condition, your opponent's condition, and your game plan are all worth thinking about during a match. The time to do that thinking is between points and games, not while the ball is in play.

Become as totally absorbed as possible in the match you are playing. Try to isolate your playing from the rest of your life for the short period of time you are on the court. Forget for a while that many other things in your life are more important than playing a game. If you can (and want to), create a temporary attitude in which the next point, game, or set is more important than family, friends, or society. If you set that attitude of pure focus as a goal, any progress toward it should improve your game by sharpening your concentration.

Mental Focus Drill 1. *Silent Practice*

Practice tennis strokes with a partner for 10 minutes without saying a word. Allow nothing to distract you from hitting the ball. Agree ahead of time on the practice routine to be followed. Any combination of strokes can be used.

To Increase Difficulty

- Increase the length of silent practice to 15 minutes.
- Play an entire set without talking, except to announce the score.

To Decrease Difficulty

- Break the silent practice session, or aim for shorter talk-free segments.

Success Check

- Avoid talking.
- See the ball; hit the ball.

Score Your Success

1 to 3 minutes of silence = 1 point

4 to 7 minutes of silence = 3 points

8 to 10 minutes of silence = 5 points

Your score ___

Mental Focus Drill 2. *Deuce Games*

Deuce games and tiebreaker matches, the next drill, are designed to help you concentrate under pressure. In deuce games, play a set in which every game starts with the score at deuce. Play the ball, not the point or the other player. If weather conditions are not a factor, change sides after you have completed five games.

To Increase Difficulty

- Start each game down 30-40.

To Decrease Difficulty

- Start each game at 30-30.

Success Check

- Make each game last at least 4 more points.
- Get the ball in on every first serve.

Score Your Success

0 to 2 games won = 1 point

3 to 4 games won = 3 points

5 to 6 games won = 5 points

Your score ___

Mental Focus Drill 3. *Tiebreaker Matches*

Play three consecutive tiebreakers. Scoring is based on the number of times you win the tie-break game.

To Increase Difficulty

- Start each tiebreaker down a point.
- Start each tiebreaker down 2 points.

To Decrease Difficulty

- Start each game up a point.
- Start each game up 2 points.

Success Check

- Make each game last at least 4 more points.
- Set goals of 70 percent of first serves in and first serves returned.

Score Your Success

1 tiebreaker won = 1 point

2 tiebreakers won = 3 points

3 tiebreakers won = 5 points

Your score ___

Mental Focus Drill 4. *Goal Setting*

This exercise is called *goal setting.* Award yourself 5, 7, or 9 points, depending on how many goals you achieve during one set. Goals are to hold three serves or win three games the first time you have a game-point opportunity or to win the first point of at least three games. Practice one goal at a time.

To Increase Difficulty

- Increase the goal by one.

To Decrease Difficulty

- Decrease the goal by one.

Success Check

- Set realistic goals.
- Review goals during changeovers.

Score Your Success

0 to 2 held serves = 5 points
3 to 4 held serves = 7 points
5 or more held serves = 9 points
Your score ___

ATTENTION CONTROL

Regardless of the playing condition that threatens your concentration, attention control has been described as the single most important factor in the performance of world-class tennis players. Two sport psychologists at Brunel University in England, Dr. Costas Karageorghis and Professor Peter Terry, suggest that the following skills can sharpen athletes' ability to control their attention:

- Focusing on a specific object or player
- Focusing on one's thoughts or feelings

- Blocking out irrelevant information
- Controlling emotions
- Memorizing routines
- Using cue words

In *Sport & Medicine Today,* Karageorghis and Terry also describe eight exercises to help players improve their attention control. These exercises are described in table 11.1.

ADJUSTING TO OPPONENTS

Whether you play recreational or competitive tennis, you will come into contact with many different kinds of opponents. Some will try to hit the ball hard right at you; others will try to be sneaky and get the ball past you. Some you will enjoy playing against and others you will not. Whatever the case, you need to be able to adjust your game to take advantage of your own strengths and your opponent's weaknesses.

Big Hitters

There are two kinds of big hitters. The first kind of big hitter executes heavy serves, powerful groundstrokes, put-away volleys, and strong overhead smashes. They like to serve and rush the net, and they like to hit forcing groundstrokes. Their asset is power. Their weaknesses may be a lack of patience, consistency, and sometimes mobility. It is difficult to hit consistently powerful shots for an entire match. Watch for these weaknesses, and be ready to take advantage of them. Most important, don't allow yourself to be intimidated. These big hitters can be beaten, even if they look good while they are losing. Use these strategies against this kind of a big hitter:

- Make returning first serves a priority.
- Buy time by playing a step or two deeper to return serves.

Table 11.1 Concentration Activities

Activity	Description
Use verbal cues.	Use words or phrases that will trigger performance in specific situations. Decide which words will work for you. Some tennis examples are "eyes up" during the serve, "hold tight" on volleys, "hit through the ball" on groundstrokes, and "light touch" on drop shots.
Identify distractions.	On one side of a sheet of paper, write down relevant details of the elements essential for good performance. On the other side, list possible distractions such as crowd noise, weather, and other competitors. Awareness of potential problems can help you develop a strategy to cope with them.
Replace thoughts.	Practice replacing negative thoughts with positive ones. Instead of thinking, *The wind is going to be a problem,* think, *How can I get an advantage with the wind?*
Capture the image.	Find an object or image, and practice focusing attention on it for as long as possible. Use a stopwatch to measure progress.
Center yourself.	Between points or during changeovers, focus attention on the center of the body as you breathe in a slow, deliberate fashion. With practice, centering can have a calming, controlling effect on performance.
Have a routine.	Have a game-day routine that begins in the morning and continues right up to the minute a match starts.
Test your concentration.	Enlist training partners to try to distract your attention during a crucial part of an event. Having someone talk or move while you are hitting or playing is a good test of concentration.
Pull the trigger.	Do something to direct your attention toward the impending action. Get into a crouch just before a service return. Perform a last-minute stretch before the start of a match. Mimic the movement of the arm before a serve.

- Return serves to your opponent's feet when he or she rushes the net.
- Attack second serves when the opportunity presents itself.
- Shorten your backswing when returning power shots.
- Do not fight power with power.
- Slow down the match.
- Keep the ball deep in your opponent's backcourt.
- Don't panic when you are occasionally overpowered. (See the take your best shot drill.)
- Use the offensive lob, especially early in the match.
- Use two shots—low setup, then a winner—to pass a player at the net.
- Hit some shots directly at the power player.
- Set a goal of extending each point beyond four shots.

- Anticipate your opponent trying to hit crosscourt for winners.

The second type of big hitter uses power strokes from the baseline, but is not necessarily that good or that interested in playing at the net. Try these tactics:

- Hit a quality first shot to take charge of the point.
- Try not to give your opponent his or her favorite shot.
- Hit short occasionally to force him or her to come to the net.
- Experiment with hitting serves and groundstrokes directly into the body.
- Vary the pace, spin, and location of serves.
- As much as possible, dictate the course of the point rather than reacting to what your opponent does.

Big-Hitter Game Drill.   *Take Your Best Shot*

Play 10 points in which you set up your practice partner with his or her favorite can't-miss, finish-the-point shot. Count the number of points out of 10 you win; then change roles.

To Increase Difficulty

- Allow your opponent to use the doubles alleys.

To Decrease Difficulty

- Score a point when you return the first shot.

Success Check

- Anticipate the direction of the shot.
- Execute a quick first step to get to the ball.

Score Your Success

1 to 3 points won = 3 points

4 to 7 points won = 5 points

8 to 10 points won = 7 points

Your score ___

Retrievers (Pushers)

It can be very frustrating to play retrievers—players who get everything back but with little pace. They are certainly not intimidating players, and they probably won't impress you with their strokes. If you watch these counter-punchers warm up or play against someone else, it is easy to become overconfident.

The problem is that the ball seems to keep coming back no matter how well you play. These players know their capabilities, and they play within their limitations. In practice, try the plan a point drill. Here are some ideas on how to play these human backboards:

- Make the retriever come to the net.
- Be aggressive when possible.
- Attack the second serve.
- Avoid playing the retriever's style of tennis.
- Stick to your game plan, but play with patience.
- Respect the retriever as much as any other kind of opponent.
- If you have a choice, avoid playing a retriever on a slow court.
- Anticipate the need to hit one extra shot to win the point.
- Plan on long matches.

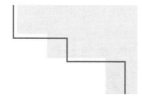

Misstep

You fail to recognize your opponent's style.

Correction

Use the warm-up or first two games to assess your opponent.

Retriever Game Drill.   *Plan a Point*

Play 10 consecutive points and change serves after 5. Plan the first three shots of every point (for example, serve, approach, volley or crosscourt forehand, crosscourt forehand, down-the-line forehand).

To Increase Difficulty

- Allow your partner to serve every game.
- Score a point only if you win the game.

To Decrease Difficulty

- You serve every game.
- Plan only the first two shots of a point.

Success Check

- Focus on your first shot of the exchange.
- Use a variety of plans.

Left-Handed Players

Left-handed players have an advantage in tennis. The percentage of successful left-handed players seems to be disproportionately high. No one is used to playing left-handers, and few people enjoy the experience. Crucial shots seem to go to the left-handed player's forehand. It can take a whole set to figure out their serves. If it makes you feel better, left-handed players also don't like to play against left-handed players. Try these tactics to overcome the left-hander's natural advantages:

- Regroove your strokes to avoid hitting to the forehand side.
- From the right side, serve wide to the left-handed player's backhand.
- Most of the time, serve down the middle from the ad court.
- Anticipate that the left-handed player's serve will spin to your left.
- Realize that normal put-away shots might go to the left-handed player's strength.

Superior Opponents

Once a match begins, try not to worry too much about how good your opponent is. You are stuck with each other, so go ahead and play your style of game. If you are afraid that every shot by your opponent will be a winner, you will play below your capability. Try to relax a little and play each point rather than worrying about the outcome of the match; you may play even better than you normally do. Superior players frequently bring out the best in inferior opponents. Simulate this situation with the 0-40 drill (page 140).

Sooner or later, every tennis player has to compete against someone with superior talent. But going against someone who is physically superior doesn't have to result in an automatic loss. Following are strategies for winning regardless of the matchup.

First, observe your opponent. Even elite athletes have weaknesses. Andre Agassi couldn't volley well. Pete Sampras couldn't win big matches on clay courts. Serena Williams couldn't. . . . Okay, this is a bad example. Lesser athletes have to look for the few deficiencies that great athletes possess. By observing, making mental notes, or just asking questions, you can "steal" points, games, and matches by exploiting minor weaknesses.

Second, work hard. Physical prowess comes easily to gifted athletes. But that doesn't mean the rest of us can't master sport skills. It just takes us longer to reach the same level. Some children learn to read quickly; others require more time and effort. But the end result is that both groups can read. If you can't match your opponent's natural physical skills, you may be able to make up the deficit by outworking him or her during practice sessions.

Third, learn to anticipate. Athletes who are a step slower than world-class athletes can make up some of the difference in quickness and speed by anticipating what is about to happen. A tennis player starts moving to either the forehand or backhand side in anticipation of where the next shot will be hit. Anticipation is a great equalizer, although it's difficult to quickly acquire the ability to know what is about to happen. This skill takes intelligence, experience, and the physical ability to act on what you observe.

Fourth, try to gain control. The worst mistake an underdog can make is trying to play the type of game preferred by the superior athlete. You can't beat a baseliner by outlasting him on groundstrokes. Shorten points by getting to the net or making him get to the net. Play within your physical limits. One hundred percent of your limited ability may be enough to beat a star who plays at 80 percent of perfection.

Fifth, try to survive. Whether it is by skill, guile, luck, or perseverance, your goal is to survive and stay close to the talent-heavy favorite as long as possible. If the score is close near the end of the match, it doesn't matter who has the most talent. The person who wins is often the one who makes a big shot, avoids a mental error, is in better physical condition, or just gets lucky. In these situations, physical talent is not a prerequisite.

Finally, endure. Superior athletic talent does not necessarily carry over from one age group to the next. The person who was physically superior at 20 may not be the same athlete at 30, 40, or 50. Older, in some cases, however, really is better. The less-than-elite athlete who trains and plays long enough may emerge as the winner later in life.

When all the elements needed to be successful in sports are equal, superior talent will win. But, things are seldom equal. Sometimes the less-talented tennis player can find ways to win by doing all of the little things the supertalented athlete often neglects.

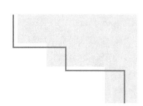

Misstep

You fail to make adjustments to your game.

Correction

Use the 90-second changeover to think through a change in tactics.

Superior-Opponent Game Drill. *0-40*

In the 0-40 drill, play a set in which every game is started with the score 40-0 or 0-40 against you. Test your ability to maintain concentration and poise when coming from behind.

To Increase Difficulty

• Allow your opponent to serve every game.

To Decrease Difficulty

• Retain the choice to serve or receive serve every game.

Success Check

• Concentrate on returning every first serve.
• Play each point—not the game, not the set.

Score Your Success

1 to 3 games won = 5 points

4 to 7 games won = 7 points

8 to 10 games won = 9 points

Your score ___

Weaker Opponents

Keep your focus sharp even if you are playing someone you should easily beat. Be nice, but try just as hard to win every point as you would against someone who is your equal. If you can win 6-0, do it. Never throw points or games in a match because you feel sorry for the person on the other side of the net. Save your compassion for social tennis. When you are comfortably ahead, work on weak areas of your game but not at the risk of losing momentum. If an opponent cannot challenge your tennis skills, make the match a challenge to your concentration. The handicap scoring drill will help maintain your competitive edge.

Weaker-Opponent Game Drill. *Handicap Scoring*

Play a set in which the player behind by one game begins the next game ahead 15-0. If losing the set by two games, the losing player begins the next game ahead 30-0. If losing the set by three or more games, the next game begins at 40-0.

To Increase Difficulty

- The person losing the set gets a choice of serving or receiving every game.

To Decrease Difficulty

- The person winning the set never starts a game behind by more than 2 points.

Success Check

- Be aggressive when down in the score.
- Maintain concentration regardless of the score.

Score Your Success

Winning a set 6-4 or 7-5 = 3 points

Winning a set 6-2 or 6-3 = 5 points

Winning a set 6-0 or 6-1 = 7 points

Your score ___

Jerks

Some players may deliberately try to distract you or interrupt your thinking with an assortment of unsportsmanlike behaviors. Some of the more popular methods are stalling, talking to you or to spectators, arguing, being overly dramatic, and giving you a bad call just to upset you.

You can handle these situations two ways without totally losing concentration. The first is to decide that nothing an opponent can do will bother you. If you expect trouble from an opponent or even if you get it unexpectedly, make a conscious decision that you will retain your poise and concentration regardless of what happens. Doing so is a difficult task, and it becomes even more difficult if you are losing. Then, even minor irritations become magnified. It is a lot easier to

concentrate when you are winning than when you are losing.

If peaceful coexistence is unfeasible, you might as well confront the person and try to solve the problem before the match continues. Don't put up with distractions if worrying about them is going to interfere with your game. If you are thinking about the distractions, you are not thinking about tennis. Stop the match, call your opponent to the net, and explain what is bothering you. If you don't get any cooperation, ask for an umpire or get a ruling from the tournament referee, if there is one. If the match is supposed to be merely a social one, do a better job of selecting opponents next time. It's not worth the hassle.

Jerk Game Drill. *One Free Cheat*

Play a set and allow your opponent to make one deliberate bad call during the set. The "free cheat" may be used at any time, regardless of the score. Your assignment is to retain your poise in spite of being cheated and to continue playing as if nothing unusual is happening.

To Increase Difficulty

- Allow your opponent two free cheats per set or one per game.

To Decease Difficulty

- Allow both players one free cheat per set.
- Do not allow a free cheat on a game point.

Success Check

- Show no reaction to the bad call.
- Maintain focus.

ADJUSTING TO CONDITIONS

Just as every opponent will be different, so will every environment in which you might play a match. The type of court you are playing on, the weather conditions, and various outside distractions will all affect your game. It's important to learn how to adjust to different playing conditions. The tips in this section will help you adjust for different court speeds, windy conditions, extreme temperatures, and noise so that every game you play will be an enjoyable experience.

Court Speed

The casual tennis fan may not know it, but court speed—how the surface of a court affects the bounce of the ball and its velocity after the bounce—determines the outcome of many tennis matches. Many of the great clay-court (slow surface) players of the world do very poorly on slick, fast courts. And some great fast-court players (Pete Sampras, for example) never win a major title on clay courts. Good tennis players can adjust to any kind of surface, but it takes time. Following are some tips to adjust your game to both fast and slow courts.

Going to a fast, slick court is particularly difficult because on these courts the ball skids and bounces low. If you have to make an adjustment, try to schedule some practice time on the court before match day. The entire pace of the game is faster. Shots seem to be hit harder, rallies are shorter, and less time is available to get into the rhythm of the match. Try these fast-court tactics:

- Turn your shoulders quickly, get the racket back early, and start your swing early.
- Rely less on full-body rotation to prepare for groundstrokes.

- Use the open stance as much as needed on groundstrokes.
- Play deeper than usual, especially on the serve return.
- Make returning first serves a priority.
- Block hard serves defensively.
- Return serves low and at the feet of a net-rushing server.
- Apply less spin on serves.
- Go to the net on medium-deep shots you would not normally follow.
- Expect your opponent to be more aggressive than on slow courts.
- Bend your knees and stay low to hit groundstrokes.
- Don't overhit setups.
- Attack all short balls without overhitting, and hit them behind your opponent.
- Volley aggressively to the open court with angled shots.
- Rely less on topspin and more on flat and slice groundstrokes.
- Expect short rallies.
- With more downtime than on slow courts, work to maintain concentration.

Adjusting to a slow court is much easier than adjusting to a fast court. On slow, rough courts, the ball slows down and bounces higher than it does on fast courts. Instead of having less time to prepare for shots, you will have more than enough time on a slow court. You will not be able to put shots away as easily, and you may become impatient because the points last longer. Retrievers love these courts, and power players detest them. Everyone can win a few more points by trying these slow-court strategies:

- Assuming you are comfortable with these grips, use western and semiwestern grips on high-bouncing groundstrokes.
- Use a bigger backswing to generate power.
- Apply topspin to create high bounces.
- Hit groundstrokes with an open stance, if necessary.
- Be more deliberate than on fast courts.
- Rely more on serve placement, spin, and pace than on power.
- Be selective about when to advance to the net.
- Do not underestimate the retriever on a slow court.
- Improve your physical stamina.
- Be patient.
- Expect long rallies.

Wind

Problems created by playing in the wind can be approached two ways. The first is to dread the whole experience, complain about conditions, and blame poor play or losses on windy conditions. The other approach is to try to use the wind to your advantage. When the wind is in your face, it can keep shots in the court that would normally go out. When the wind is at your back, it can add pace to average or weak shots, and it can cause more trouble for your opponent than for you. The trick is to become so involved in the match that you don't even worry about the wind. These strategies will help you deal with windy conditions:

- Choose to play against the wind in the first game of a match.
- Toss the ball lower on the serve.
- Keep lobbing to a minimum, especially when playing against the wind.
- Play closer to the net when the wind is against you.
- Play more aggressively when the wind is against you.

- Let the wind provide some of the power on your strokes.

Extreme Temperatures

It would be nice to play all matches in 68-degree, 50 percent humidity weather, but that rarely happens. Serious players have to prepare for competition in an extreme climate as if it were another opponent. They acclimate themselves to the temperature as much as possible, wear the proper clothing, eat and drink the right foods and fluids, and pace themselves to endure difficult situations. The ones who are successful turn the obstacles of extremely hot and cold weather into assets.

Prepare for playing in extreme heat as if preparing to play a tough opponent. Don't ignore the problems hot weather can create. Players who try to prove how tough they are run the risks of cramping, dehydration, fatigue, and not being able to hold onto a sweat-covered racket during long points. When playing in extremely hot weather, remember these keys:

- Don't wear yourself out trying to serve hard, especially on slow courts.
- Make your opponent move around the court.
- Conserve energy between points.
- Take the full 90 seconds on changeovers.
- Keep your racket grip dry with towels, wristbands, and drying agents.
- Alternate rackets often enough to keep the grip dry.
- Dress comfortably and coolly with loose-fitting tops.
- Wear light-colored apparel that won't absorb the heat.
- Drink cool water or sport drinks before, during, and after a match.
- Sit in the shade between points and games.
- Keep ice or an ice pack at courtside, and put it on your neck during changeovers.
- Wear a hat.
- Use sunscreen and reapply it often.

Playing in cold weather is not as bad as it seems. The body has a remarkable capacity to warm up quickly. Once you get into the flow of a match or practice session, the cold temperature is not really a serious factor. Cold weather combined with strong winds is another story. Here are some suggestions to help you adjust to cold-weather conditions:

- Dress in layers and shed clothes as the exercise intensity increases.
- Take as much time as allowed to warm up.
- Don't take the full 90 seconds on change-overs unless you need it.
- Use a cut-out sock or glove on your dominant hand to keep it warm.
- Wear a hat or cap to prevent heat loss.
- Drink fluids (warm, if desired) to stay hydrated.

Noise

Noise can be distracting if you are not used to it. If people are making enough noise to warrant a legitimate complaint, either tolerate it or ask them to be quiet. If the noise is coming from traffic, from work being done near the courts, or from passersby, learn to live with the noise or choose a quieter place to play.

Actually, once you learn to play with a lot of noise, your concentration should improve. If you can concentrate in noisy areas, you should be able to concentrate even better in quiet surroundings. Players who learn to play on noisy public courts probably have an advantage over club players used to quieter surroundings. Some of the drills described earlier also can be effective with noise. Dealing with distractions, whether it's the other player or playing conditions, is a challenge of concentration, not tennis skills.

Boom-box tennis is an activity (not a drill) that can help you get used to excessive noise around a tennis court. Take a radio or boom box to the courts, and play a match against an understanding friend when no other players are present to distract. Turn the volume up louder than normal during the match. The idea is to maintain concentration in spite of the added noise. Show absolutely no reaction to the distraction. To increase difficulty, play a CD you don't like or increase the volume even more. Decreasing the difficulty is simple; just lower the volume.

SUCCESS SUMMARY

Skills for this step are more mental than physical, so simulating game situations is not easy. Table 11.2 lists the drills that tested your ability to manage difficult situations. Enter your score for each one in the table and total your points. A passing score is 30 out of a perfect 61.

Becoming a successful tennis player involves a lot more than just hitting the ball over the net. Playing against different players in all types of situations makes the sport even more fun and challenging. The variety also levels the playing field. It allows players with certain strengths to take advantage of them. Variety also makes it possible for weaker players to devise game plans that make them more competitive against superior opponents. When you reach a point in your tennis life where you no longer worry about stroke technique and are able to focus instead on more sophisticated elements of the game, you know you're making progress.

Remember that the title of this book is *Tennis: Steps to Success*. The word *steps* is there for a reason. Forget the big picture. The idea is to take one step at a time, building one stroke on top of another until you have a complete game—or at least a game as complete as it can be while it's under construction. Don't wait for perfection. The greatest players in the world are not perfect. They wrestle with the same problems that you will encounter on groundstrokes, serves, and net play. Along the way, you can add the extras of specialty shots, tactics, strategy, and how to handle all of the outside elements that go with the sport of tennis. With a little talent, a lot of effort, and some luck, you might be able to take your steps to success a little faster than others. Whether you go fast or slow, be sure to enjoy the ride.

Table 11.2 Scoring Summary

Mental Focus Drills

1. Silent practice	_____ out of 5
2. Deuce games	_____ out of 5
3. Tiebreaker matches	_____ out of 5
4. Goal setting	_____ out of 9

Big-Hitter Game Drill

1. Take your best shot	_____ out of 7

Retriever Game Drill

1. Plan a point	_____ out of 9

Superior-Opponent Game Drill

1. 0-40	_____ out of 9

Weaker-Opponent Game Drill

1. Handicap scoring	_____ out of 7

Jerk Game Drill

1. One free cheat	_____ out of 5

TOTAL _____ **out of 61**

◨ Glossary

ace—A winning serve that the receiver cannot touch with the racket.

ad—Advantage; refers to the point after the score was deuce.

ad court—The left half of a player's court as the player stands at the baseline and faces the net.

ad in—A reference to the score when the player serving has won the point after the score was deuce.

ad out—A reference to the score when the player receiving the serve has won the point after the score was deuce.

all—A tie score; 30 all, for example, means that the score is 30-30.

alley—A lane four feet wide that runs the length of, and on both sides of, the singles court. The alleys are in play for all shots after the serve in doubles.

amateur—A person who does not accept money for playing or teaching tennis.

angle shot—A shot that crosses the net at a severe angle.

approach shot—A shot that the hitter follows to the net.

Association of Tennis Professionals (ATP)—An organization composed of most of the leading male players in the world.

Australian doubles—A doubles formation in which the player at the net (the server's partner) lines up on the same half of the doubles court as the server.

backcourt—The part of the court between the service line and the baseline.

backhand—A stroke that a right-handed player hits by reaching across the body to the left side; a left-handed player reaches across to the right side to hit a backhand.

backspin—Reverse spin on the ball, like a car wheel in reverse.

backswing—The preparation for a stroke in which the racket is drawn back before being swung forward.

balance point—The point in the shaft of a racket where the head and the handle are balanced.

band—The strip of material attached to the top of the net.

baseline—The boundary line that runs parallel to, and 39 feet from, the net.

block—The return of a ball with a very short swinging motion.

carry—A shot that is carried on the racket strings, slung, or hit twice as the ball is returned. Carries are legal unless the player makes two or more deliberate attempts to hit the ball over the net. Carries may be called by the umpire or the player who hits the ball.

center mark—A line dividing the baseline at the center. The server may not legally step on the center mark before striking the ball.

center service line—The line in the middle of the court, perpendicular to the net, that divides the two service courts.

chip—A groundstroke hit with a short backswing and with backspin on the ball. The chip usually is meant to be a shallow shot (not very deep into the opponent's court).

choke—To play poorly because of the pressure of competition.

choke up—To hold the racket at a point higher on the handle, away from the base of the grip.

chop—A shot hit with backspin to any part of the court.

circuit—A series of tournaments at the state, sectional, national, or international level.

closed stance—A hitting position in which the foot closest to the net steps across the body toward the singles sideline instead of toward the net.

closed tournament—An event open only to players in a particular geographical area.

composite—A reference to tennis rackets made from the combination of two or more materials.

continental grip—Holding the racket so that the player does not have to change grips between forehand and backhand strokes. The wrist is placed directly over the top of the grip.

crosscourt—A shot hit diagonally from one corner of the court to the opposite corner.

cross strings—Strings running horizontally from one side of the racket head to the other.

Davis Cup—An international team tennis event for male players.

deep—A reference to the area near the baseline.

default—The awarding of a match to one player or team because an opponent fails to appear or is not able to complete a match; synonym for forfeit.

deuce—A tie score at 40-40 and each tie thereafter in the same game.

deuce court—The right half of a player's court as the player faces the baseline.

dink—A shot hit with very little pace or depth.

double fault—Failure on both attempts to serve into the proper court.

doubles—A match played with four players.

down the line—A shot hit more or less parallel to the closest sideline.

drive—A groundstroke hit forcefully and deeply into an opponent's court.

drop shot—A softly hit shot, usually with backspin, that barely clears the net.

drop volley—A drop shot hit off a volley.

eastern backhand grip—A grip in which the V formed by the thumb and index finger is above but slightly toward the left edge of the racket as a right-handed player prepares to hit a backhand.

eastern forehand grip—A grip in which the V formed by the thumb and index finger is above but slightly toward the right of the racket handle as a right-handed player prepares to hit a forehand.

error—A point lost as a result of one player's mistake rather than the other player's good shot.

face—The flat surface formed by the strings and the racket head.

fast court—A tennis court with a surface on which the ball bounces low and moves rapidly toward or away from the hitter.

fault—Failure on an attempt to serve into the proper court.

Fed Cup—An international team tennis event for female players.

feed-in consolation—A tournament in which players who lose in the early rounds of a tournament reenter the championship draw and may finish as high as fifth place.

finals—The match played to determine the winner of a tournament.

flat—A shot hit with little or no spin. Also a term used to describe tennis balls that have lost their firmness and resilience.

flexibility—How much a racket bends from head to shaft or from one side of the head to the other when contact with the ball is made.

follow-through—The part of the swinging motion after the ball has been hit.

forcing shot—A shot hit with enough pace or depth to force an opponent into a difficult return.

forehand—A stroke that a right-handed player hits on the right side of the body and a left-handed player hits on the left side.

forfeit—To award a match to one player or team because an opponent fails to appear or is not able to complete a match; synonym for default.

frame—The tennis racket, excluding the strings.

gauge—The measure of a string's thickness. The higher the number, the thinner the string.

graphite—A man-made, carbon-based material 20 times stronger and stiffer than wood; often used in rackets.

grip—The manner in which a racket is held. Also, the part of the racket where it is held.

grommet—A small, round plastic sleeve in the frame through which the strings pass.

groove—To hit shots in a patterned, disciplined, and consistent manner.

groundstroke—A shot hit with a forehand or backhand stroke after the ball has bounced on the court.

gut—Racket string made from cow or sheep intestines.

hacker—A person who does not play tennis well.

half volley—A shot hit just after the ball has bounced on the court. Contact is made below knee level.

head—The upper part of the racket where the strings are attached.

head heavy—A racket that has a balance point more than 1/4 inch from the center (midpoint of the racket's length) toward the head.

head light—A racket that has a balance point more than 1/4 inch from the center (midpoint of the racket's length) toward the handle.

hindrance—Called when a player is hindered by either an opponent or a spectator. It results in a let or a point awarded to the player hindered.

hitting surface—The flat surface formed by the strings.

holding serve—The server has won the game that he or she just served.

hook—A slang term meaning to cheat.

International Tennis Federation (ITF)—The international governing body of tennis.

invitational tournament—A tournament open only to players who have been invited to participate.

junior racket—A racket less than 27 inches long that is usually lighter than standard rackets and has a smaller grip.

Kevlar—A synthetic fiber used to strengthen tennis racket frames.

ladder tournament—Competition in which the names of participants are placed in a column. Players can advance up the column (ladder) by challenging and defeating players whose names appear above their own.

let—A serve that hits the top of the net and lands in the proper service court. Also, an expression used to indicate that a point should be replayed for any of a number of other reasons.

linesperson—An official who is responsible for calling shots either in or out at the baseline, service line, or center service line.

lob—A high, arching shot.

lob volley—A lob hit with a volley.

long—An informal expression used to indicate that a shot went out past the baseline.

love—An archaic but commonly used way to say zero in the tennis scoring system.

main strings—The vertical strings running from the top to the bottom of the racket head.

match—Competition between two players in singles, four players in doubles, or between two teams, as when two school teams complete against each other.

match point—The stage of a match when a player can win the match by winning the next point. The term is used by spectators and television announcers during a match and by players after a match. It is not, or should not be, used by the umpire or players in calling out the score.

mixed doubles—Competition pairing a man and woman on one team against a man and woman on the other team.

net game—Shots hit while playing near the net, such as volleys and smashes.

net umpire—An official responsible for calling let serves.

no—An informal expression used by some players to call shots out.

no-ad—A scoring system in which a maximum of 7 points constitutes a game. For example, if the score is tied at 3 points for each player, the next player to win a point wins the game.

no-man's-land—The area of the court between the service line and the baseline. This area is usually considered a weak area from which to return shots during a rally.

not up—An expression used to indicate that a ball has bounced twice on the same side of the court before being hit.

nylon—A strong synthetic material commonly used for racket strings.

off hand—The hand that does not hold the racket.

open stance—A hitting position in which the feet are parallel to the net.

open tennis—Competition open to amateur and professional players.

out—A call indicating that a shot has bounced outside a boundary line.

overgrip—A one-piece grip that slides over the original racket grip.

overhead smash—A hard, powerful stoke hit from an over-the-head racket position.

pace—The velocity with which a ball is hit, or the velocity of the ball.

passing shot—A groundstroke hit out of reach of an opponent at the net.

percentage shot—The safest, most effective shot hit in a particular situation.

placement—A winning shot hit to an open area of the court.

playing pro—A person who makes a living playing tennis.

poaching—When a doubles player at the net cuts in front of his or her partner to hit a volley.

point penalty—A system in which a player must be penalized points, games, or even matches for improper conduct.

power zone—The area of the racket's hitting surface that produces controlled power with no vibration (see also *sweet spot*).

professional (pro)—A person who plays or teaches tennis for money.

pro set—A match that is completed when one player or team has won at least eight games and is ahead by at least two games.

pusher—A type of player who is consistent but who hits with very little pace.

put-away—A shot that is literally put away (out of reach) from an opponent.

qualifying round—A series of matches played to determine which players will be added to a tournament field.

rally—An exchange of shots.

ready position—The position in which a player stands while waiting for a shot.

receiver—The player to whom a serve is hit.

referee—An official responsible for supervising all competition during a tournament.

returner—A player who gets everything back but does not play aggressively.

round-robin—Competition in which all participants compete against each other in a series of matches. The player or team finishing the competition with the best win–loss percentage is the winner.

rush—To move toward the net following a forcing shot.

second—An informal expression used by some players to indicate that the first serve is out.

semiopen stance—A hitting position between an open and square stance in which the feet are aligned so that the body is partially open to the net.

semiwestern forehand grip—A way of holding a racket that is approximately halfway between an eastern and western forehand grip.

serve—The shot used to put the ball into play at the beginning of a point.

server—The player who begins a point with a serve.

service break—The loss of a game by the player serving.

service court—Either of two alternating areas into which the ball must be served. Its boundaries are the net, the center line, the service line, and the singles sidelines.

service line—The line that is parallel to, and 21 feet from, the net.

set—The part of the match that is completed when a player or team has won at least six games and is ahead by at least two games.

set point—The stage of a set when a player or team can win the set by winning the next point.

shadow swing—Like shadow boxing, a practice method in which a player goes through the motions of a swing without hitting a ball.

shaft— Part of the racket between the head and the grip.

sideline—The boundary line that runs from the net to the baseline. The singles sidelines are closer to the center of the court than the doubles sidelines.

single-elimination tournament—A type of competition in which players' names are drawn and placed on lines in a tournament bracket roster. Matches are played between players whose names appear on connected bracket lines. Players who win advance to the next round of competition; those who lose a match are eliminated from competition.

slice—To hit the ball with sidespin, like the spin of a top.

slow court—A court with a surface on which the ball bounces and slows down after the bounce.

split set—An expression used to indicate that two players or teams have each won a set.

square stance—A position in which the toes of both feet form a line parallel to either sideline.

straight sets—A reference to winning a match without losing a set.

string savers—Small pieces of material that attach to racket strings to make them last longer.

stroke—The manner in which a ball is hit (forehand, backhand, volley, and so on).

sweet spot—The exact place on the racket face that produces controlled power with no vibration (see also *power zone*).

synthetic—A type of racket string made from specially designed nylon.

T—The T is the location on a tennis court where the center service line intersects the service line to form the letter T.

take two—An expression meaning that the server should repeat both service attempts.

tank—To tank a match or point is to deliberately try to lose it.

teaching pro—A person who teaches people to play tennis and is paid for the service.

throat—Part of the racket just below the head.

tiebreaker—A method of completing a set when both players or teams have won six games.

titanium—A strong, lustrous, white metal element used in small amounts in the construction of some rackets.

topspin—Bottom-to-top rotation on a ball, like a car wheel going forward.

touch—The ability to hit a variety of precision shots.

twist—A serve in which the ball's spin, imparted by the racket, is the opposite of what it would normally be. A right-hander's twist serve produces left-to-right spin on the ball.

umpire—A person responsible for officiating a match between two players or teams.

unforced error—A point lost with no pressure having been exerted by the opponent.

United States Tennis Association (USTA)—A national, noncommercial membership organization whose mission is to promote and to develop the game of tennis.

vibration dampener—A rubber or plastic device inserted at the base of the racket strings (near the throat) to reduce the vibration on impact with the ball.

volley—A shot hit before the ball bounces on the court.

western grip—A way of holding the racket in which the wrist is positioned directly behind the handle.

wide—An expression used by some players to indicate a shot went out beyond the baseline.

wide-body—A description of a racket frame with a very wide head.

Wimbledon—A tournament in England, generally considered to be the most prestigious in the world.

World Tennis Association (WTA)—An organization consisting of the world's leading female professional players.

yoke—The part of the racket immediately below the head; the upper part of the shaft; the throat.

◰ About the Author

Jim Brown, PhD, has taught, coached, played, and written about tennis for over 40 years. He has served as the editor of *Tennis Industry* magazine and the *Georgia Tech Sports Medicine & Performance Newsletter*, and is now the executive editor of the *Sports Performance Journal*, an online publication of Athletes' Performance in Tempe, Arizona. Jim has represented the United States Tennis Association; the American Alliance for Health, Physical Education, Recreation and Dance; and the President's Council on Physical Fitness and Sports in clinics throughout the United States and Mexico.

Dr. Brown has written, coauthored, or edited 11 books, two national newsletters, one magazine, and hundreds of articles on sports, sports medicine, health, and education. He writes columns for CBS Sportsline.com, USTA-Southern Section, and Senior Wire News Service. His work has appeared in such notable publications as *Sports Illustrated for Women*, *The Washington Post*, *Better Homes & Gardens*, *Raising Teens*, and *New York Post*.

Jim and his wife, Arlene, live in Atlanta, Georgia.